MORE Transforming Negative Self-Talk

MORE

Transforming Negative Self-Talk

Practical, Effective Exercises

Steve Andreas

W. W. Norton & Company
New York • London

To Milton Erickson, Virginia Satir, and Fritz Perls—and many of their students—from whom I have learned so much, over so many years. Your voices of wisdom and practical skill continue to live, echoing through time into the present, guiding me in my continuing exploration and clarification of human experience, and how to change it.

Printed in the United States of America

For information about permission to reproduce selections from this book, write to Permissions, W. W. Norton & Company, Inc., 500 Fifth Avenue, New York, NY 10110

For information about special discounts for bulk purchases, please contact W. W. Norton Special Sales at specialsales@wwnorton.com or 800-233-4830

Manufacturing by Courier Westford
Book design by Ken Gross
Production manager: Leeann Graham

Library of Congress Cataloging-in-Publication Data

Andreas, Steve.
More transforming negative self-talk : practical, effective exercises / Steve Andreas.
pages cm
Includes bibliographical references and index.
ISBN 978-0-393-70973-5 (pbk.)
1. Self-talk. 2. Negativism. 3. Criticism, Personal. I. Title.
BF697.5.S47A527 2014
158.1—dc23 2014020782
ISBN 978-0-393-70973-5 (pbk.)

W. W. Norton & Company, Inc., 500 Fifth Avenue, New York, NY 10110
www.wwnorton.com

W. W. Norton & Company Ltd., Castle House, 75/76 Wells Street, London W1T 3QT

1 2 3 4 5 6 7 8 9 0

Contents

MORE ^ Transforming Negative Self-Talk

Introduction

Your task is that of altering, not abolishing.

— *Milton H. Erickson (in Rossi & Ryan, 1986)*

Troublesome self-talk is something that we all experience at some time in our lives. But for some people it is an everyday, every-hour experience, 24-7, that even torments them in their dreams. Most people try to ignore a troublesome voice, argue with it, or even try to silence the "chattering monkey mind." However, that is a lot of work, which is mostly ineffective, and it isn't permanent. Others attempt to turn off their tormenting voices with meditation, drugs, or dangerous activities, but those methods are also temporary, only partly effective, and may have many problematic consequences. In this book I want to focus on what does work, rather than what doesn't work, so in the last two chapters I discuss how and why trying to abolish or silence a troublesome voice doesn't work.

Whether you experience a troublesome voice often, or only occasionally, wouldn't it be nice if that voice could be transformed from a ruthless persecutor into a supportive friend, ally, and trusted advisor? That may seem very unlikely, but actually it is surprisingly easy.

In my previous book, *Transforming Negative Self-Talk* (S. Andreas, 2012) I presented a wide variety of very simple and rapid ways to change a troublesome voice and your response to it. For example, you can change where you hear the voice coming from in your personal space, hear it farther away, change its volume, tempo, or tonality, add background music or a song, and so on. You can use these methods without regard to the voice's content (the words that the voice speaks) making them useful exercises with any voice, no matter what it says. You can also use these methods without exploring the origin of the voice in your personal history.

Often one or more of these methods will be enough to change your experience of a voice for the better. Sometimes these changes offer temporary relief; sometimes they will be more lasting, but in either case they are practical and empowering; they give you tools that you can use any time you choose to.

However, while these simpler methods provide some relief, some improvement in how you feel, you may desire more change.

In this book, I build on this solid foundation and develop more comprehensive ways to transform a troublesome voice. When you make a change that takes into account the larger context in which the voice is speaking, the consequences of the voice's communication, the voice's positive intent, and so on, it is much more likely to fit well with the whole of your experience. Because this embraces more aspects of your experience, the changes tend to be more lasting, and the benefits of the changes will tend to spread more widely throughout your life. In the first three chapters I explore a number of different useful individual processes, and then combine them into a longer sequential process (Chapters 4, 8, and 9) for even deeper and more lasting transformation. This complete process is illustrated with several verbatim transcripts of actual therapy sessions, each of which includes different examples of how to utilize the key principles embedded in the process.

Listening to a Voice

If people in the real world say something that upsets or troubles you, and you try to ignore, silence, or attack them, that usually is not very useful or effective. Others will usually redouble their efforts to be heard and get you to understand, or they may attack in return. If you are in a position of power, you may be able to silence them, but they will still oppose you, and probably try to get back at you in indirect ways. Since a troublesome internal voice is an echo of your experience of someone in the real world, it will respond in much the same way.

But if you listen to someone carefully and try to understand what he or she is saying, including the messages embedded in the nonverbal aspects of the voice, you have at least some chance to come to a mutual understanding. When you really listen to the qualities of what a voice says—its tonality, tempo, and music—you can discover additional messages that you didn't hear before.

For instance, a mother who says, "Don't stay out past 10!" can easily be understood as meaning that she still thinks of you as a small child who can't be trusted, and that she wants to control your every move. But if you listen to the strained quality of her voice, you can realize that it expresses her uncertainty, her fears for your safety, and the love and caring that gives birth to her strident words of caution. You may even come to realize that what you thought the words were saying is not what she meant at all.

When you really listen to a brother's voice that is continually putting you down, you can realize that he is feeling inferior to you, and that he is desperately putting you down as a way of trying to correct this imbalance. Each bit of additional information enriches the words, and often it will change the meaning entirely, sometimes even reversing it, as when you realize that the words are spoken in a tone that indicates sarcasm.

Every internal voice is a brief echo or sound bite of some interaction that you had with someone in the real world, even when it sounds like your own voice. But this echo is usually only a very tiny part of the larger experience in which it occurred. Often a voice will be that of a family member or someone else whom you know well, and with whom you have an extensive history. When you have listened carefully to a voice, and determined whose voice it is, that opens up all the information in your past experience of this person, providing a richer context to what the voice says and giving it a fuller meaning.

Often what a voice says is only a conclusion about experience, one of many possible conclusions that could be drawn from that experience. When that conclusion becomes separated from the experience it arose out of, it is easy to think that it is the only valid conclusion. When you explore the larger historical context of the voice, and hear that voice within that context, it is possible to see the big picture, providing a much broader perspective. You can realize that any experience can be understood in a variety of ways, opening up additional choices that can spontaneously change your response to a voice in the present.

When you join with an internal voice, befriend it, and work toward understanding it better, you can establish a more positive relationship with it. It will become much more cooperative and willing to adjust what it says to you and how it says it. Although it may seem unlikely to you, it is even possible to make peace with a troublesome voice, and then negotiate with it and transform it, so that it speaks to you in ways that are much more pleasant, helpful, and useful. There are many different elements that can support you in accomplishing this, and the first few chapters of this book explore some of the most important ones. The brief summaries below outline what lies ahead in each chapter.

1. Joining With a Voice

I begin by exploring how to join with an alienated voice. That is not something that most people would think of doing. Most people (and most books about how to deal with troublesome voices) tell you to avoid or counter what the voice says. Why join with a voice that criticizes and torments you, making you feel bad?

However, joining with an opponent is a fundamental principle in all the Asian martial arts—aikido, judo, tai chi, and so on. When you join with the force that is attacking you, two things happen: (1) you are no longer the target of the attack; and (2) you are now in a position to gently redirect the force and protect yourself from harm. The same is true of joining with an internal voice that is attacking you.

2. Retrieving and Clarifying Information

Next I explore how to ask an internal voice questions—just as if it were another person in the real world—in order to retrieve additional information and clarify the meaning of what the voice says. I explore how using the familiar—and overlapping—questions who, where, when, what, and how can be used to enrich a sound bite that tortures you into a much fuller and more complete experience. Knowing who is speaking provides a wealth of background information about the underlying attitudes and perceptions, biases, and limitations. Where this occurred provides additional context, an important factor in creating meaning. When this occurred, and what happened before and after that, expands what you are able to notice. What else was happening at the time the words were said provides a fuller understanding, and the question how reveals the actions that were going on at the time between all the who's and the what's. All of this provides more of the big picture in both time and space.

3. Asking for the Positive Intent

Next I explore the assumption that every communication has a positive intent. A father's criticisms and suggestions about how you could do better can easily be understood as his being disappointed in you or not liking you. When you realize that these criticisms arise out of his loving you and wanting you to do well in life, that completely changes the meaning of his words. You may still wish that he would communicate with you in more positive ways, but your relationship will change, and it will be much easier to think of him with good cheer instead of irritation, anger, or despair. "Oh, there he goes again. He just never learned how to offer advice gracefully. He knows that others are likely to take offense at his suggestions, so he tries to cover up his uncertainty with gruff bravado."

Understanding a voice's positive intent makes it very easy to join with it. You can realize, "I'm glad my father loves me and cares about my well-being," while at the same time wishing that he could change how he expresses this caring. Positive intent is a very powerful fulcrum that provides leverage to change behavior. A possible response is, "Hey, Dad, I get that you love me and want me to do well in life; it would be really helpful if you would first ask me if I want suggestions, and when I do want them, to offer them in a softer and more loving tone of voice."

4. Putting It Together

Chapter 4 demonstrates how to put the different processes described in Chapters 1 through 3 together into a unified sequential process of self-discovery. The transcript is from a recorded teaching demonstration at a Milton Erickson Brief Therapy Conference, where different approaches to therapy are presented and demonstrated. When I teach a process like this, I almost always teach without any information about its content—the words that the voice is saying—for several reasons. First, allowing demonstration subjects to keep the specific content to themselves preserves their privacy; they don't have to reveal any information that could potentially result in self-consciousness, embarrassment, or other distress. Second, this makes it very clear that the process can be used with any voice, and that the content is not necessary in order to guide someone in using the process. Third, students aren't distracted by thinking about the content, because none is revealed. This allows full attention to learning the steps in the process and how those steps are communicated. The transcript is followed by a detailed outline of the process.

5. Listening for an Underlying Problem

A verbatim transcript of another therapy session shows how working with a troubling voice can become an entryway to an underlying problem that requires a different specific method for resolution. In this example, the troubling voice expresses depression in response to the death of a loved one and the resulting feeling of emptiness, loss, and sadness. This requires going beyond simple changes in the voice itself to having a dialogue with the dead person, in order to reconnect with him emotionally. This is a process for resolving grief that goes far beyond typical grief work, which usually only involves expressing the feelings of loss fully.

6. Making Use of a Voice's Special Abilities

In this chapter I explore how you can make use of a voice's unique perceptions, skills, and abilities to expand your own. What is this voice really good at, and when and where could this voice be useful to you? You can learn how to enlist this voice to spontaneously coach you and guide what you do in specific contexts, in order to make your life better. If a voice is particularly good at small talk, it can take over when you find yourself with nothing to say in social situations. If a voice is really good at perceiving flaws in communication, it can be a primary resource to you in a wide range of situations, from listening to a sales pitch to esoteric academic discussions. Perhaps a voice is only useful to you in deciding which shot to take in a game of pool, but why let this resource remain unused?

7. Using the Voice of a Trusted Friend

Think of a trusted friend whom you would listen to willingly, no matter what he said, or how he said it, and listen to the special qualities of this voice—the unique tonality that allows you to identify this friend on the phone after only a word or two. As you listen to this voice, you can realize that the tonality conveys an enormous number of positive presuppositions, attitudes, and implications. You know that this friend cares for you and always wants the best for you. If the voice that troubles you used this tone of voice, you would always be willing to listen to it attentively—which is what the voice itself also wants. You can ask a troubling voice if it would be willing to adopt this voice tonality of your trusted friend, so that you would always be happy to listen to it, no matter what it said.

8. Putting It Together—Again

In Chapters 6 and 7, two additional processes have been presented and discussed—making use a voice's special skills and using the voice of a trusted friend. The transcript presented in Chapter 8 includes these additional aspects of transformation to support and amplify the previous process, and uses it to create an even more comprehensive package of experience that will be durable and lasting.

9. Putting It Together—in a Different Way

A transcript from a hypnotherapy session shows how all the different principles discussed in this book can be found in a session that on the surface might appear to be very different, in both style and sequence, from what I have presented. The methods and principles offered in this book are presented in the form of a specific sequential outline for the sake of clarity and easy learning. Like learning to playing scales on a musical instrument, it is a way to make your skills spontaneous and automatic. However, when you have learned scales well, you can then use those skills to play any kind of music, and also to improvise new melodies. Once you have thoroughly learned the basic principles presented here, you can use them freely whenever they are appropriate.

10. Protecting Yourself From External Voices

Most of this book is directed at troubling internal voices that are echoes of interactions you have had with real people at some time in your life, many of which were intrusive, troubling, or destructive. If you had been protected from these external voices at the time, you wouldn't have internalized them, and you wouldn't need to read this book to find out how to transform them. This book would be incomplete without teaching you how to protect yourself from intrusions from the voices of others in the present moment—how to decide for yourself whether or not the views and opinions of others are worth taking in and considering, so that you are no longer a helpless victim of whatever someone else says.

11. Not Talking Back

Many books and authorities—some of them very famous and well respected (and well paid)—tell you to argue and fight back against a troubling internal voice, but this is rarely useful. Most of this book is devoted to what does work—listening to, adjusting, and working cooperatively with a voice. However, since opposing a voice is so widely taught and accepted, I need to provide a detailed discussion of the problems created by talking back to a voice, and how it usually only makes a bad situation worse.

12. Not Silencing an Internal Voice

Recognizing that internal voices are often troublesome, many spiritual teachers advocate silencing internal voices. Some of these teachings are thousands of years old and have been adopted by tens of millions. However, since most internal voices are useful most of the time, this is truly throwing out the baby with the bathwater. Like fighting back against a troublesome voice, trying to silence it altogether is doomed to frustration and failure, again making a bad situation worse.

1. Joining With a Voice

Before we explore what it means to join with a voice, and how to do that, I want to offer an example of how to join with someone else you are in conflict with. If you have ever been in an argument (in contrast to a friendly discussion) with someone, you know how easily that can degenerate into an acrimonious and endless battle, and how seldom it results in a satisfactory resolution of your differences. The true story below by Gerry Schmidt, a therapist, offers a very unusual and interesting alternative to conflict.

Closing Together[1]

It was the summer of 1992, the last day of a residential training in the Rocky Mountains in Winter Park, Colorado. A group of 75 people had bonded very strongly over the past 20 days, and one thing they did as part of their group process was to create a piece of visual artwork representing "our community" or "who we are." The group started with a big sheet of plywood, which they covered with a collaborative painting symbolizing their experience together. It was painted with red, white, black, and yellow to symbolize all the peoples of the earth, and it was filled with a collage of handprints, spirals, a yin/yang symbol, and the individual contributions of every participant. The finished piece was very meaningful to everyone.

Now we were at the very end of a packed three weeks and the group was about to finish their time together and head home. Only one thing remained to be done. The question before the group was, "What are we going to do with this piece of art that is 'us'?" The group discussion started, and since I was the closing trainer I was somewhat involved with helping facilitate this process. Soon it became clear that most of the group's opinion was that it should be kept safe and given to somebody who would be the custodian. But the question remained, "How the heck are we going to do this?" We had people from all over the world, and it was not a small piece of plywood. Who was going to take it and how were they going to get it there?

Then one man spoke up.

"Well," he said, "because this is so challenging, and because we're spread out all over the planet—we've got people from Europe and Asia—my proposal is we destroy it. If we burn it, it will be like everybody has it."

I could feel the tension in the room mount instantly. It was clear that the group was generally very opposed to the idea of destroying it. It was the end of 20 days, and everyone was tired and ready to leave. I could see in their faces that to most of them, burning the artwork would seem like a great offense to what it represented. The man who had offered the sugges-

1 From *Sweet Fruit from the Bitter Tree: 61 True Stories of Creative and Compassionate Ways Out of Conflict* by Mark Andreas. © 2010, by Mark Andreas. Real People Press, pp. 280–284. Used by permission.

tion was thinking on a more abstract level, but most everyone else wanted to preserve this piece of art that represented the close-knit community they had formed over the past weeks. They did not want it destroyed.

I was trying to facilitate the conversation but despite a lot of training and experience in conflict resolution, I was not particularly effective. After about 15 minutes we hadn't made any progress toward a solution. I had my eye on the clock because we were already going overtime and I needed to get everybody out of the room. It was obvious to me that this was not going to resolve quickly. Even on the "keep it" side there were many different opinions, but that side was becoming more and more polarized against this guy who was saying, "destroy it." People were getting frustrated and upset, and the prospect of a satisfying group closing was unraveling by the second. At this point somebody in the group stood up and proposed to have a vote at least to get past the "keep it" or "destroy it" alternatives. But before I could respond, a Native American from the MicMac tribe in eastern Canada stood up and faced me directly.

"Gerry, can I take over?" He asked. "I have an approach, and if you give me ten minutes by the clock, I'll have it solved."

I had absolutely no idea what he had in mind, but I was more than glad to have him take this problem off my hands. I was tired and the discussion wasn't going anywhere useful, so I told him to go ahead.

He came up to the front of the room and first he asked, "Everybody's agreeing that we're ready to get a resolution?" People nodded, so he continued. "I have the solution if you're all willing to go along."

Everyone said, "Yeah, yeah, go ahead."

Then he turned to the man who wanted to destroy the artwork, and gesturing to him he spoke in a soft, deep voice that seemed utterly unconstrained by time.

"In my Native American tradition, when we have a group which is all on one side, and we have one person who is on another side, we would never have a vote to overrule him, because it's obvious that the majority will win, making him isolated. We would never do that to someone.

"The solution is we're going to turn over the responsibility for the decision to you—the one who's the isolated person. We're going to let you decide for all of us."

There was no mistaking that the words of the Native American were wholeheartedly genuine and sincere. He was really completely giving over the decision to this man.

I could hear people's jaws hitting the floor, and as I looked around the room I saw eyes wide with surprise. It was an amazing thing to watch the wave of shock move through the room. But then very quickly I began to see that certain people started to understand the wisdom in what he had done, and they relaxed a little.

The man who had been given responsibility to make the

decision went through his own initial shock. Right at first there was a little bit of glint in his eye, a hint of power and triumph. But then I saw changes taking place inside of him as well. His face went through several emotional swings, though I couldn't tell exactly what they meant. Then he stood up to speak.

"Well I think it's obvious that we need to find a way that satisfies all of us," he said.

I could feel the tension in the room disappear. Earlier it had been clear in the man's argumentative tone that he had set himself against the rest of the group, but as soon as the responsibility was completely in his hands, his resistance simply melted away. It was wonderful. He immediately started moving in the other direction.

"My objection was that there wasn't a place where we could put the artwork," he said, "And I want to honor the spirit of what we all did together. Is there a place where we could put this piece of art where everybody would have access to it, and it would feel fair to all of us?"

Very quickly someone who had not been involved in the earlier discussion spoke up. "I have a place," she said. "It's a big barn in the central US where I could hang it. I also have a truck here; we could cut the piece in half to transport it, and once it's hanging up I can take a picture of it and send it to everybody, and anyone can drop by and visit it at any time."

Immediately it was done. The shift was profound. The emotional ripple that swelled through the room was huge. You can tell the difference between people who are just agreeing because they want an argument to be over, and people who are deeply and fully satisfied. It was quite a wonderful moment. Everybody was really pleased, including the man who had originally objected. The whole group was suddenly aligned and there was a powerful sense of completion.

I think part of the reason it worked so well was because the guy who was given the responsibility had such a strong relationship with the group. The wisdom of the Native American in trusting so much responsibility with this one man made me imagine a culture in which that kind of approach was a common practice. That conception of community would create a profoundly different way of working together.

My MicMac friend looked at his watch and said, "Seven minutes." (M. Andreas, 2010, pp. 280–284; used by permission)

Giving the responsibility for the decision about what to do with the artwork to the lone dissenter was a way of allying with him, saying in effect, "We trust you to make a good decision about this," eliminating the disagreement between the dissenter and the rest of the group. When he no longer needed to defend his position against the group, the dissenter could incorporate the group's thinking into his own, and he became much more reasonable. The result, which seems paradoxical, was that the decision was satisfactory to both the dissenter and the group.

When you have an internal voice that troubles you, that voice is a recorded echo of difficult interactions you have had with others in your personal history, sometimes called an "old tape loop." Accordingly, a troublesome internal voice will behave in much the same way as those people in your past. If you argue with it, or fight it, or try to not listen to it, or eliminate it, it will usually fight back vigorously, just as someone in the real world would. But if you take steps to befriend a troublesome internal voice and ally yourself with it, you can develop a more positive relationship with it, and begin to move toward resolution of your differences. Joining with a voice can be a very useful first step toward really listening to it, understanding it and how it functions. This approach is something that very few people would ever think of doing on their own, but it has some very interesting consequences. The example below of treating a lawyer's insomnia is from Douglas Flemons, a brief therapist in Florida.

> Clients come for therapy because some chunk of their experience is happening outside their conscious control, and it's driving them—and/or someone else—crazy. The brief therapy work I offer employs the logic and methods of hypnosis to invite a reunion between their conscious intention and an automatic and alienated part of the self.
>
> Brian, a high-powered trial lawyer at the top of his game, was desperate about his insomnia. He got five to six hours of sleep on a good night; two to three—or none at all—on a bad one. And for the last few years, most nights had been bad. He'd tried everything, from warm milk and various medications, to relaxation tapes and hypnosis, but nothing had worked. When he'd lie down to try to go to sleep, a five-to-ten second auditory "loop" would form in his head—the chorus from a pop song, a snippet of conversation from earlier in the day, a snatch from a trial—and torture him for hours on end. Despite making formidable efforts, he could never get the loop to stop. After a couple of hours of tossing and turning, he would roam the house, looking for some magic location that might afford him some relief. But the longer sleep eluded him, the more agitated and strung out he'd become.
>
> Brian had a reputation for being relentless. If purposeful effort could achieve a goal, he'd apply himself with the focus of a laser beam. But this skill, which worked so well in the courtroom, backfired when he tried to implement it at bedtime. He couldn't make himself fall asleep and he couldn't successfully will the loop in his head to stop. It wasn't because he wasn't trying hard enough, but because, given the nature of consciousness, he was trying too hard.
>
> I asked him if he could get a loop started as he sat there in my office. Having never tried to create one on purpose, he was

a little surprised at my suggestion, but he was willing to give it a shot. Within a few minutes, he had one going full tilt in his head, so I moved into hypnosis and offered the following suggestions:

"While that loop continues, repeating over and over, you can listen to it with the back of your mind, and to me with the front of your mind. Or you can follow the loop with the front of your mind, while the back of your mind monitors where I'm headed. It doesn't really matter. You might even find them switching back and forth.

"This morning at breakfast, I told my 6-year-old daughter, Jenna, to quit dawdling. 'Finish up your cereal, Honey,' I said. She looked at me with a twinkle in her eye and said, matching my tone of voice, 'Finish up your cereal, Honey.' 'Hey, what are you trying to pull?' I joked, to which she replied, 'Hey, what are you trying to pull?'"

"I complimented her on how well she was able to imitate not only my words, but also the tonal quality of my voice. She smiled at this, so I asked whether she could repeat what I was saying while I was saying it. As I said, 'I hope you have a good day at school, Sweetheart,' she looked intently at my mouth and managed to form each of the consonants and vowels of the words just a fraction of a second behind my articulating them. I found myself slowing way down as she spoke almost in unison with me, and at the end of the sentence we both burst out laughing.

"A funny thing happens when you have two or more people voicing the same thing at the same time. If you're in a choir, holding a certain note, and everyone around you is singing the same note, then the boundary separating you and them dissolves, and your experience of yourself melts a little. You and the other singers blend together.

"I wonder what would happen if the front of your mind were to 'pull a Jenna' and start imitating, in unison, that back-of-your-mind loop? Instead of trying to stop it, it could create an exact replica, so you'd have two loops going, the automatic one that you can't get to stop, and a deliberate one, giving you a stereo experience. Go ahead and try that, and let's see what happens. Match the voice or voices in speed, articulation, accent, volume, and tone.

"When both are in unison, you may not be able to tell if the deliberate loop in the front of your mind is following the automatic one in the back of your mind, or if the automatic one has synced up with the deliberate one. Both can move together, in unison, around and around, giving you that stereo experience."

I continued on in this vein for a while, and when I checked in with him, Brian told me that the loop had gradually faded out—something that had never happened before.

In asking Brian to initiate a loop, I helped him connect with something automatic that he'd always tried to eradicate. By helping him shift his intentionality, I helped relief and sleep to develop spontaneously. By inviting him to purpose-

> fully imitate it, I facilitated a dissolving of the boundary between his conscious intention and his symptom—a previously alienated part of his experience.
>
> Later in the session, I taught him a self-hypnosis technique to use at night, and suggested that he practice "singing in unison" with whatever loops appeared at bedtime. He came back two weeks later, having slept well almost every night, and he no longer felt trapped by the automatic workings of his mind. He liked the irony, he said, of feeling empowered by not doing anything to the loops. We did some fine-tuning of his self-hypnosis, and he left, able to sleep and no longer at war with himself. (Flemons, 2004, pp. 43–46; used by permission)

How does joining with a voice work? At the simplest level, if you have a muscle that twitches involuntarily—like an eyelid tic or a twitch—you can attend to it and deliberately twitch it voluntarily until you can do it in exactly the same way. By doing this, you can gradually discover exactly which muscle is twitching, and which nerve is stimulating the muscle to twitch. Eventually this can bring the autonomous twitch under conscious control again.

The same principle works with our thoughts, which are also elicited by our movements. If Brian had matched the voice in his head out loud, it is obvious that he would have used the movements in his throat, mouth, and lips, and the breathing movements that support speaking. When he did this internally, he did the same thing, but not as obviously. In order to think a thought, you need to move some muscles.

The same thing happens with images, which are also a part of your thinking, as you can easily discover for yourself. Try the following little experiment. Close your eyes, and place a hand on your head in some way, and notice the image that you have of the position of your hand. Now move your hand, as if gently stroking or massaging your head, and notice how the image of your hand changes spontaneously in response. . . . [2]

Now keep your hand motionless while still in contact with your head, and try making the visual image of your hand move, but without actually moving your hand. . . .

Most people find this very difficult, if not impossible. Now try something a little different. Put your hand in your lap, or somewhere else, and imagine that your hand is stroking your head in the way it did before, and notice how your image of your hand moves. . . .

For most people this is much easier, because when your hand is somewhere else, there is more contrast between your imaginary movements and the feelings that you are actually getting from your

---

2 Three dots (. . .) indicate a pause to do the action described and discover what you experience. You will learn fully from this book only if you pause for a few moments to try each little experiment.

hand. When you imagine moving your hand, that activates many of the same nerves and muscles that you use when you actually move your hand, and the image of your hand moves in response to these implicit movements. Brain imaging studies confirm that this kind of process underlies most—and perhaps all—of our thinking. Joining with an autonomous voice, as Brian did, uses the same kind of process to reunite with it and gradually discover what nerves and muscles are involved—in this case the muscles of the throat that produce sound—and bring it back under voluntary control.

Exaggeration

Another way to join with a voice is to not just echo it, but add to what it says, exaggerating the message, either by making the words stronger and more emphatic or by increasing the volume, the tonality, or any other nonverbal aspect of the voice—or all of them at the same time. If a voice says, "You sure messed that up," you can say, "Boy, I sure did; I not only messed that up, I screwed up my whole life!" in a voice that is louder and in a tonality that is more disgusted, despairing, or authoritative than the original. Like a caricature, this emphasis can bring into awareness aspects of the communication that otherwise might be ignored. Exaggerating what the voice says will often elicit a spontaneous opposite-polarity response such as, "Well, it isn't really that bad."

When you initially do this, there may be no change in your response, or it may even make you feel worse. But if you continue to do this, you will usually find that you don't take it quite as seriously as you originally did. Paradoxically, joining with an internal voice and exaggerating what it says often results in diminishing your feeling response to it. You may even come to think of it as silly or ridiculous. Pause now to identify an internal voice that has criticized you, and listen carefully to what it says, including the volume, tone, tempo, and so on. . . .

Next, exaggerate what the voice says, by changing some of its nonverbal aspects, as we explored in detail in my previous book, *Transforming Negative Self-Talk* (S. Andreas, 2010a). Increasing the volume, using a more authoritative tonality, or speeding up the tempo will make the message stronger and more forceful. . . .

Different people will find that different aspects of this exaggeration will be more impactful for them than others. If you experiment a little with the same voice in different situations, or with different voices, you may find that you only need to exaggerate the words, or the volume, or some other specific aspect of the tonality or tempo in order to get a useful change in your feeling response. Once you have discovered what works well for you, you will have found a shortcut, something you can easily do any time you want to change your experience of a voice.

Discovering Assumptions and Attitudes

Another way to deepen your understanding of what a voice is communicating is to discover the underlying assumption or attitude in what it is saying, and exaggerate that instead of the voice itself. Often we aren't actually responding to the words but to an underlying belief that we may not be noticing.

For instance, when an event doesn't immediately satisfy our wants or desires, it is easy to jump to an inner voice that says, "Damn it!" or "That stupid—" directed toward the event, or to other people involved, responding with disappointment, frustration, blaming, anger, or even violence. When we do this, we aren't really responding to the event itself, but to an implicit assumption that we should be satisfied, and right away. "I deserve it!"

Occasionally someone else may have made an agreement with you and then broken it. But more often we think the world owes us something just because we exist—or because we have worked hard, or because we are rich, or important, or beautiful, or some other rationale.

If you exaggerate this underlying assumption, you can often elicit a useful change in your response. In this kind of situation I have found it useful to say to myself—in a fast, imperious, demanding, and petulant voice—"I want what I want, when I want it—NOW!"

That exaggeration usually brings a smile, or a chuckle, and a more balanced perspective on whatever it is that seemed so vitally important to me at the moment. If not, a few repetitions, perhaps louder or more strident, will usually succeed.

Exaggeration is one of the principal methods used by Frank Farrelly in his *Provocative Therapy* (Farrelly & Brandsma, 1974). He joins with and exaggerates the client's problem to outrageous proportions. For instance, he may join with what an alcoholic is already saying to himself: "You'd be nuts to change and become sober! As it is you have a universal excuse for any mistake you make—it was the bottle. You don't have to take responsibility for anything; if you want a break from that boring job or your nagging wife, you can just go on a bender, and no one can blame you, because you just have a disease. Being an alcoholic isn't a problem—it's a solution! You've got it made." Exaggeration usually elicits an opposite response; thinking of all the drawbacks of being an alcoholic may elicit renewed motivation and commitment to change.

In the next chapter I explore how to ask a voice for more and fuller information, in order to further enrich our understanding of what it wants to communicate. The more information you have, the more you can begin to move toward resolving whatever is troubling you.

2. Retrieving and Clarifying Information

One of the most interesting and useful aspects of a troublesome internal voice is that you can communicate with it in exactly the same way you would with someone else in the real world around you. You can ask it or tell it literally anything, and receive a response. Most people either just listen passively to an internal voice, or they try to argue or fight with it. If you argue or fight with it, that will have the same kind of results that it has in the real world: contention and conflict, but seldom any resolution. In fact, that will usually make the internal voice even stronger and more oppositional. Even if you are successful in shouting it down and overcoming it, that won't really eliminate it permanently—it will come back to haunt you. Misunderstanding is the food of conflict; if you want to reduce the conflict between you and a troublesome voice, more information will bring deeper understanding of what the voice is really trying to say to you.

In Chapter 1 I showed how listening to a voice and joining with it can be quite useful. Now I want to use this as a starting point and foundation for doing something even more important. Rather than thinking about a troublesome voice as an enemy, you can think of it as if it were a friend who isn't very good at communicating. Instead of trying to struggle with it, fight it, or run away from it, you can learn to join with it, listen more carefully to what it is saying, and find out more about it. When you really listen to a voice, and speak back to it respectfully, it will gradually become more reasonable, and you can begin to learn more about it.

Of course, just as in the real world, you may not initially receive an answer, particularly if your relationship with the voice has not been very good. If you have fought with it for years, or tried to eliminate it, it may initially be very antagonistic and not want to talk to you at all. For instance, when one man first tried to communicate with a troublesome internal voice, the answer he received was a very loud, "Screw you!" When he continued to speak to the voice in a friendly way, gently requesting an explanation, the voice replied, "You have completely ignored me for twenty-five years—and now you want to talk to me? Screw you!" This may not seem like a very auspicious beginning, but it did provide some understanding, and an opening that could be developed into a deeper understanding.

Apologizing

When someone in the real world is antagonistic, and you want to ally with him or her to find out more about what is going on, it can be very useful to apologize sincerely—even when you don't know what you are apologizing for. When the other person understands that you sincerely regret the miscommunication between you and that you want to make amends, he or she is much more likely to communicate in a reasonable way and be more open to explaining.

When an internal voice is antagonistic, the situation is exactly the same. You can explain that you have only just learned that it is possible to communicate directly with it, and ask it to please forgive your past stupidities. If you continue to speak to it respectfully, eventually it will answer you, and you can begin to have a more friendly and informative dialogue that clarifies what the voice wants to communicate.

Facts and Conclusions

When an internal voice criticizes you, reminds you of past mistakes, failures, or other unpleasant events, that voice is usually stating a conclusion based on some event or set of events. What the voice says is seldom a fact; more often it is an opinion, a generalization, or a judgment about an event. Often the information about the event that the opinion is based on is completely omitted from the statement itself, and the conclusion appears to be an established fact, rather than an opinion.

Since a fact seems to be absolutely true, when the "fact" is unpleasant, it can seem to you as if nothing can be done about it. If your conclusion is different than the voice's conclusion, you have a stalemate, with no chance of agreement. But if you explore the event that these different conclusions are derived from, you have a chance to find a basis for agreement.

For instance, when a voice says, "You're stupid," or "I'm stupid," that is not a fact; it is an opinion about some event that is not mentioned at all. It is easy to conclude that the word "stupid" applies to everything you do, everywhere, throughout all time, extending inexorably into your future. If you really are stupid in all contexts, then there is probably nothing you can do about it, so it's natural to feel very bad—or even depressed or suicidal.

The actual event that the opinion is based on might be a single event, like having done poorly on a test in a class. Furthermore, it might be that you didn't have time to prepare, you were sick, or you forgot that there was a test, or you had some other reason for doing poorly. If that was the case, not only was it a single isolated event, it had nothing to do with being stupid; it had to do with being too busy, or forgetful, or even something like getting sick that was completely out of your control. When you examine the event carefully, you can often discover that the conclusion that an internal voice makes about it is inappropriate.

Even when a voice mentions a specific event, such as, "I can't believe you said that to her last night; you're really insensitive," that still brings up only a very small part of what actually happened, namely one sentence that you said to someone else during a very short period of time. When you review all the other information about that event—all the other things you said and did, who else was there, what was happening, how you felt at the time, and the larger context, all of that adds to your understanding. If you examine all the things you said that evening, you may find that except for that one sentence, you were exceptionally sensitive to others. More information always leads to a more balanced response.

Fortune-telling

There is one kind of conclusion that is particularly difficult and discouraging. Often a voice will take a past event and cast it into the future as a prediction. Not only did you fail in the past, you will fail in the same way in all contexts in the future. This kind of prediction may sometimes be your own conclusion about some event, but very often it is word for word what someone else said to you. Either way it is making an unwarranted assumption that you will be the same in the future as you were in the past, presupposing that you can't change.

When you only hear a voice and its conclusion, that omits all the information about the speaker, what happened at that time, how that person was feeling, and the larger context in which those words were spoken. All those elements contribute to the meaning of what was said. Recovering this additional information often changes the meaning of the event, so that you can come to a different conclusion, and a different response to it.

For instance, one man's internal voice originated from his father, who often criticized and put him down for what he did. When he saw his father's face, he could see the worry lines that indicated that his father was really concerned about him and wanted the best for him. That completely changed his response to what his father said.

Retrieving Information

Missing information can be divided into five major categories, and we can recover it by asking the familiar questions that we use to gather information about any event: who, where, when, what, and how.

You may have noticed that the question why is not included in this list. Why is much less useful, because it doesn't elicit information about the event itself, but about someone's understanding or conclusion about the event. Asking why would usually only take us back to the conclusion that we have already made based on limited information, so that wouldn't change the meaning of what the voice says. Our goal is to gather more information in order to find a more useful conclusion.

Let's examine each of the questions in turn. Although each question directs our attention to a somewhat different aspect of your experience, you will find that they usually overlap. When you ask who, you will probably also recover information about where, when, what, or how as well—and that will be true of each of the questions. The only reason for asking each question in turn is to make sure that you examine all the different aspects of an event thoroughly, in order to recover as much information as possible.

As you ask yourself the questions below, it is important to notice what your internal experience is. It is not necessary to answer the questions verbally, either internally or out loud. In fact, if you answer them verbally, that will tend to divert your attention from your experience, and it is this experience that can enrich and change the meaning of an internal voice. The questions are only useful ways to direct your attention.

Who

Who spoke those words to you in the past? One of the most useful pieces of information that you can retrieve is the identity of the voice, because that is often the doorway to a wealth of information. If you listen very carefully to the sound of the voice—the tonality, volume, and tempo—you can first determine if the sound indicates that it is your own voice, or someone else's.

Someone Else's Voice

When you identify the source of this voice—who said this to you—that makes available a flood of information about the speaker: age, background history, attitudes, motives, interests, beliefs, intentions, relationship to you, and so on. All this information provides a much richer context for the meaning of the words that the voice says, and this often spontaneously changes the meaning.

For instance, if the voice belongs to someone who was competing with you, what it says may only be a way to feel superior. If it is someone who is often sarcastic, what it says may be the opposite of what it really means. The words that a voice says are only a very small part of the meaning; the nonverbal aspects carry much more information and have a stronger impact.

Your Own Voice

When you hear this voice in your own tonality, you can discover the origin of this voice. "Okay, it's my own voice. Who did I learn this from? I'm sure that when I was very small I didn't say this to myself, because when I was an infant, I couldn't understand or speak any words at all. I had to learn language from others around me. Who spoke those words to me in that way in the past?"

Sometimes when it is your own voice, it is because you made a conclusion about some event. Someone else may never have said this sentence to you; that person did something—perhaps numerous times—and you drew a conclusion from that event or series of events. You can still explore the origin of this conclusion you have made, and find out who was the source of your conclusion, and what he or she did to elicit that. For instance, one woman's sentence was, "You're not good enough" (S. Andreas, 2010). Her mother had never actually said that to her but she had frequently made comments about how the daughter could do better, and the sentence was the daughter's conclusion about what her mother had said.

If you have difficulty identifying the origin of a voice, you can ask yourself, "If I did know, who would it be?" Once you have an answer, you can retrieve all the information about that person. This can be useful even if you are still uncertain about who the speaker actually is. The person that comes to your mind will not be an accident; even if your choice is wrong, it will have many of the same elements and aspects as the correct choice, so you can learn almost as much—or sometimes more—than if it was the correct person.

Much of this information that you elicit from this kind of exploration might be very hard to put into words, because it involves many responses that you may be relatively unaware of. This additional information often spontaneously changes the meaning of what the voice says. "Oh, he was always insecure; he said that to try to maintain his authority," or "She was always anger looking for a place to happen; it really didn't have much to do with me."

Visual Information

Now see the face of that person as he or she speaks to you. Once you know who is speaking, you can add a visual image of that person's face talking to you—something that often happens spontaneously as soon as you identify who it is. When you can see all the information in the visual image as the voice talks—the posture, facial expression, head tilt, and so on—that further clarifies and specifies the meaning of what the voice is saying.

Adding the nonverbal visual information of the speaker is a pure process intervention, because the instruction to see a visual image along with the voice doesn't specify anything about the content of what you will see when you do that. The content emerges entirely out of your own experience, both conscious and unconscious.

When one man added an image of the speaker's face to a troublesome voice, he was surprised to see that the face looked a bit sheepish, indicating to him that the speaker didn't really believe what he was saying. This completely changed the meaning of what the voice said, and his emotional response to it changed.

Where

Where is this event taking place? What is the larger context? Where an event takes place is a major determinant of its meaning.

If you tell a racy joke at a bar, that is likely to have quite a different meaning than if you told the same joke to your girlfriend's mother. If you expand your attention to include the larger context surrounding the event that the speaker is experiencing, that often changes the meaning of what was said, and you can reach a different conclusion. "We were just leaving church, and Mom was really concerned about what others would think about what I had done; if we had been at home, she would have said something very different."

When

What was the time frame of this event? Was it a short momentary event that you recall as a still picture, or a longer movie? Was it a single event at one time, or a series of similar events that occurred during a much longer period of time? What happened in the past that is relevant to the events at that moment, and what happened afterward as a result? Often we remember a very short slice of time, and ignore all the other events that occurred before and after. A movie provides much more information than a single still image, and you can always turn a still image into a movie that includes what preceded and followed the still image. If you expand your attention in time to include what happened previously, and what is likely to happen next, that gives you much more information to understand what the speaker said. What events is that other person responding to, either in the past or the imagined future? "She lost three family members in car accidents; that's why the idea of my learning to drive is so terrifying for her."

What

What else was happening at the time that the voice originally spoke to you, that you may not have been paying attention to at the time? Without this information, it is easy to think that what the voice says is exclusively about you and your behavior. In fact, what someone said may be primarily—or even entirely—in response to their own frustration or difficulty in responding to what just happened, or what they imagine would happen in the future as a result. "Oh, that was just after he lost his job, and he didn't know if he would be able to get another. He felt as if both his manhood and his future had just been stripped away; that's why he spoke to me like that."

How

How were you speaking, and how were you acting at the moment that your voice is commenting on? How were you feeling at that moment, and how were other people feeling and acting? "How" includes all the different aspects of process—how the "what" is happening. "We were at dinner with his colleagues, and he was talking rapidly, focused on showing off how intelligent he was; he wasn't really paying attention to anybody else, and that's why he ignored me, and dismissed what I said."

When you expand your attention in these ways to recover the who, where, when, what, and how, you can discover an enormous wealth of additional information that makes your experience of what the voice says richer and more complete, and this usually gives you a different perspective that changes the meaning of what the voice says.

When you discover a new meaning as a result of doing this kind of questioning, that is *far* more convincing and impactful than if the same shift in understanding were offered to you by someone else. There is no need for someone else to convince you that this different perspective is valid, because it arises completely out of your own experience. When your new meaning is accompanied by a sense of surprise or astonishment, that makes it even more impactful, memorable, and convincing. Now let's put this into a sequential outline.

Retrieving Information Outline

This is a pure process instruction that you can use in order to discover new meanings in what an internal voice says. Or you can offer it to someone else to enrich his or her experience. Each step provides an opportunity to come to a new understanding, and you will often find that the meaning of the voice changes, either subtly or more significantly. However, if a step doesn't offer you any new information, there will be no change in your response, so different people find different steps to be more significant to them than others.

If you do this by yourself, you will need to pause after each step to do what the outline asks you to do, and then read the next step. Then you will need to reenter your experience of the previous step before doing what the next step asks you to do.

If you know someone else who is willing to read each step to you, you can close your eyes and fully attend to your experience throughout the process, undisturbed. You won't have to be distracted by having to open your eyes to read the next step. All you have to do is indicate when you have completed each step with a nod or a brief "OK," and your guide can read the next step to you.

1. "Remember a troublesome voice, and listen carefully to what it says to you—the volume, the tonality, the timbre, the hesitations, and so on." . . .
2. "Who is speaking? If it sounds like your own voice, who did you learn from in order to speak to yourself in this way, or whose actions were the source for a conclusion that you

made?" . . . "Once you have identified the source of this voice, see the face of that person as he or she speaks to you, and review everything you know about who that person is—his or her attitudes, beliefs, likes and dislikes, skills and limitations, and so on." . . .

3. "Where are you? Expand your attention to the surroundings, the larger context in which this person—or your own voice—is speaking to you. Notice all the things and events that are close by, and also the larger landscape in the background." . . .
4. "When did this event occur? If it is a still picture, expand it into a movie that includes past events that have an influence on what is happening, and also extend this to imagined future events that have an impact on what is occurring now." . . .
5. "What else is happening in this moment? What more can you notice and learn about this event?" . . .
6. "How is this other person responding to all these factors, and how are you responding to the person? Again, notice all you can about this event." . . .

With all this additional information, it is very unlikely that the meaning of what the voice says is still the same. It is possible that the meaning changed somewhat at several—or even all—of the different steps in this process, or some steps may have been much more impactful than others. Pause now to fully notice and absorb whatever meaning the voice has for you now. . . .

Clarifying Meaning

Now you probably already have a much fuller understanding of what the voice is trying to communicate, and the meaning of what the voice said is probably already significantly different. Sometimes this also spontaneously results in changing the words that the voice says, or the volume or tone of voice that it uses.

Even if you now believe that you have a good understanding of what the voice was saying, it can be useful to go further by asking the voice to clarify its meaning, in the same way that you might ask someone in the real world, and then listen attentively to what it says in reply.

You can say, "Would you please clarify your message, so that I can understand it better? If you had been able to express all your experience of this situation—your feelings, your hopes, your fears, your understandings, your concerns—and express yourself more fully, what would you say to me now? What do you really want to say to me?" . . .

Whatever response you get, thank it sincerely and fully for responding. "Thanks very much for telling me this." . . .

If what the voice says is still puzzling, or seems incomplete to you, you can ask it to please clarify the communication further. "I'm still not clear about what you want to tell me, and this puzzles me; can you please clarify further?" . . .

Each time you receive a reply, thank the voice for responding. You can ask again as many times as you need to in order to fully understand what it wants to communicate to you.

As you follow this process of retrieving and clarifying what this voice is saying, you may discover its positive intent in speaking to you—what it wanted to achieve. Hearing a voice yelling at you is not pleasant, but understanding that someone loves you and wants to protect you gives an entirely new meaning to the same harsh words. Discovering the positive intent of a voice is a particularly important and powerful way to clarify the meaning of a communication, so I explore this in more detail in Chapter 3.

3. Asking for the Positive Intent

The old adage "The road to hell is paved with good intentions" points out that there is often a huge difference between what people want to accomplish, and what they do to try to accomplish it. What a voice tells you may be so destructive that it is very hard to imagine that it could have a positive intent, but there will always be one. For instance, a voice that tells you that you are a failure may want to avoid further disappointment; if you believe you are a failure, you won't attempt anything, and that will protect you from additional failure. A voice that tells someone to commit suicide usually wants peace that will bring an end to the suffering, which is positive. Death is not the goal; it is the means to the end.

You can ask any voice for its positive intent and get a useful answer—even if you don't know whose voice it is, your history with it, its limitations, or what the larger context is. Whether the answer that you receive is clear or vague, familiar or surprising, it offers a much more useful way of understanding the meaning of what a voice says.

For instance, if a mother yells at her daughter, that behavior is unpleasant for both of them, and it can seem as if the mother hates the daughter. But understood in the light of the mother's positive intent to protect the daughter from danger, the same behavior takes on an entirely new meaning. The yelling is still unpleasant, but now it has the additional meaning that she loves the daughter and wants to protect her.

If you first go through the process of retrieving and clarifying information described in Chapter 2, the positive intent of a voice may already have become obvious, and you may not even have to ask for it. But if not, discovering a voice's positive intent is a very useful next step. In this chapter I presuppose that you have already joined with a voice and gathered more information as described previously, so that you already have a lot of background information and can now focus your attention on how to learn more about the positive intent.

When people in the real world speak to you, they have some kind of intention, or they wouldn't bother to speak to you at all. That intent could be to tell you something vitally important, or it might only be small talk with the intent to establish or maintain a relationship, so the content of what they say might not really matter. The intent might be to remind you of something that you could otherwise forget, or it might only be to express frustration. The intent could be to communicate something that is important to you, or only to the speaker, or to both of you, or to someone else altogether. So there are different kinds of positive intent, and it is useful to be able to understand them more fully.

A very interesting experiment is to notice what you might say to someone else, but delay saying it out loud and notice what your positive intent is. If you think about offering information, is your intent simply to be useful to someone else, or is your intent to impress by showing what you know, or do you want to top what someone else has said? If you ask a question, do you really want the answer, or do you just want to demonstrate interest in what he or she has to say? This experiment is easiest to do in a group, because you can do this internally while others are speaking, and you can take your time before speaking aloud. Make a mental note to do this at your next opportunity, and you can learn a lot about your own intentions.

Since we learn to speak to ourselves by listening to others around us, our internal voices also have a variety of intentions. Sometimes those intentions may seem very negative—to punish you, scold you, or demean you, or simply to make you feel bad. However, if you ask a punishing voice what its positive intent is, you can always eventually find something useful that you can agree with.

For instance, let's take a fairly extreme example, an internal voice that tells someone to commit suicide—something that most people would agree is very negative. If you ask this voice what its positive intent is, it may initially respond that it wants to punish you for all the bad things that you have done, another negative intent. When the first response is also something negative, you simply accept it, and ask for the positive intent behind that. "OK, you want to punish me. What is your positive intent in doing that?"

The voice might then respond, "I want you to realize how stupid you are," another negative intent.

"OK, you want me to realize how stupid I am. What is your positive intent in doing that?"

When you continue this process, eventually the voice will respond with some kind of positive intent, for example, "I want to end your suffering so you can feel at peace," which is positive. I have used an extreme example to illustrate the process of continuing to ask for a positive intent until you find it. If you keep asking about a negative intent, you will always eventually find a positive one.

Usually this process is far simpler; you will often hear a positive intent the first time you ask. For instance, a voice that says, "You're stupid" may have the positive intent of getting you to study harder so that you will become more successful. Or its positive intent might be simply to express frustration that you are not doing well, something that many parents experience out of their caring for their children and wanting them to succeed.

Now I want you to discover the positive intent of a voice that troubles you in some way. First listen to what it says to you, and how it says it. Remember that I am assuming that you have already gone through the process of enriching your experience of this voice as described in Chapter 2; if you haven't done this, please back up and do this first, so that you will benefit fully. . . .

Then ask it for its positive intent, speaking to it as if it were someone else: "What is your positive intent in saying this to me?" Pause to listen for an answer. . . .

It is very important that you actually ask this question of the internal voice as if it were another person, and also that you pause and listen to what the voice actually says to you in response, in order to get access to unconscious information.

Some people will try to consciously figure out what a voice's positive intent is, but this willonly tell you what you already know, so it will usually be much less informative, and it is much less likely to be accurate. When someone answers very quickly, without taking the time to actually ask the question internally and pause while listening for a response, that is usually an indication that the person is answering for the voice intellectually. When this occurs, you can ask what the person did internally, and redirect him or her to actually ask the voice, and pause to listen to how the voice responds.

Sometimes someone will persist in responding with conscious ideas, instead of reporting a response from the voice itself. He or she may say something like, "Well, I think its positive intent is—" Then you can say, "Well, OK; please tell that voice what your understanding is, and ask the voice to tell you clearly whether or not you are correct." That accepts the conscious response, rather than redirecting it or challenging it, while at the same time insisting on clear confirmation—or disconfirmation—from the voice itself.

If the voice confirms that your understanding is correct, that's fine—conscious minds aren't always wrong. If the voice disconfirms the conscious intent, you can ask the voice again, and find out what the voice says. Or you can state another conscious guess and ask the internal voice if that is correct, until you get a clear confirmation.

When you are surprised or puzzled by how a voice responds, that indicates that the voice's response is quite different than your conscious understanding—an excellent confirmation that you have actually received an answer from an unconscious aspect of yourself.

Once you have found a positive intent behind what a voice says, that is something that you can agree with. That agreement completely changes your relationship with the voice. You are now in full alliance with the voice's intent, even though the communication itself may still be unpleasant, abusive, or destructive. Now you and the voice can work together to change what the voice says, and how it says it—and even when and where it says it—so that its behavior is more aligned with its positive intent. For instance, a critical voice may be telling you what not to do, and its intent is to improve what you do. Asking it to tell you what to do instead of the mistake you made will be much more useful.

Different Kinds of Positive Intent

It is useful to realize that inner voices can be driven by different kinds of positive intent, and that each one brings about a somewhat different kind of shift in understanding. Sometimes the positive intent of a voice was only for a parent's self-image or status—he or she didn't want to be embarrassed by others' dislike of your behavior. For instance, a parent may not dislike a child's behavior, but scold a child for doing it because others might disapprove of it, in order to be seen as a good parent.

I once had a brief conversation with a woman in her late 40s at the end of a conference presentation, and afterward I wrote down our exchange while it was still fresh in my mind. It illustrates the kind of rapid resolution that positive intent often brings, even without the detailed retrieval and clarification of information discussed in Chapter 2.

Woman: I've been wanting to write a play, but I think, "What if nobody likes it?"(When someone speaks in "quotes," a question or statement that is complete, and that has a pause before and after it, that is usually a very good indication that the person is actually hearing an internal voice speaking.)

Steve: Who is saying that to you?

Woman: My husband says that. "What if nobody likes it?"

Steve: OK, don't write the play for him. (The implication is that she can write the play for those who will like it.) Of course some will like it and some won't. (This divides the universal generalization "nobody" into two smaller categories.)

Woman: Ohhh. Some people will not like it. (Her shoulders lower a bit, she breathes out, and her chest relaxes.)

Steve: What does your internal voice say now?

Woman: "Nobody will like it."

Steve: OK. That's a little different. (Now it is not a question about a possible response, but a definitive statement about what will happen.) Listen to the tonality and tempo of that voice. . . . Whose voice is it now?

Woman: It's my parents' voices.

Steve: Good. See their faces as they say this, and then ask them, "What is your positive intent in saying this to me?"

Woman: They want to prevent my embarrassing them.

Steve: OK. How about you? Are they concerned about your not being embarrassed?

Woman: No, not me, just them.

Steve: So their communication really had nothing to do with you; it only had to do with them. So you can leave that to them. . . .

She relaxed further, and reported that her image of her parents' faces spontaneously retreated into the distance, becoming smaller. As she said this, she gestured with both hands in front of her, palms facing outward, moving away from her face to show how their faces moved away—no longer "in her face." This spontaneous change in her internal experience was a nice unconscious confirmation that she had made a useful change in understanding that would last. This little exchange took only about 3 minutes—which ought to count as brief therapy.

Often a voice only wants something positive for you, so that you can have a better life. The intent of a voice that criticizes is to identify shortcomings so that you can improve on them and become more capable. At other times an inner voice may be driven by a combination of these two intentions—parents may sincerely want a better life for their child, and may also want to maintain their self-image as good parents. At other times, a voice may have a positive intent for someone else who was affected by something that that you did. Furthermore, the positive intent can either be a relic from the past or apply to the present moment—or both. Let's examine these different kinds of intent more carefully.

A. The intent of the voice in a past external, real-life situation.

1. The positive intent is limited to the goals and outcomes of the voice speaking. For instance, the voice is only focused on its need to express frustration or anger, or to maintain its self-image or status, and so on, and doesn't even consider the impact of what it says on the listener's feelings, needs, and such. This is often true of a past voice that intrudes into the present.

   When you recognize that the voice is speaking out of its own very limited world, that means that what it said really had nothing to do with you; it was only about the voice, and you become free of whatever it said—you're no longer the target.
2. The voice has positive intent for the listener, but the voice is limited in its ability to communicate. For instance, a parent is concerned about a child's safety, but communicates this by yelling harshly and saying the child is stupid for running into the street. If you have children, you can probably think of many times when your communication with them was something less than ideal, and other times when it was very poor. If you don't have children, you can think of similar situations in which you wanted to warn or protect someone else. You had positive intent for someone, but you expressed it poorly because of your inability to be clear, or because of your emotional state, or because of some other personal limitation you had at that time.

   Another common pattern is for a parent to tell a child what not to do, while not saying what to do instead, leaving the child punished and clueless about what he or she can do to please the parent.

3. The positive intent was not for you or for the speaker, but for some other person. For instance, you were criticized or punished because your behavior kept a baby from sleeping, or you were too rough for someone who was ill or weak, or an older person.

B. The intent of an internal voice in the present, mirroring the kinds of situations described above.

1. The positive intent of an internal voice is to protect you. For instance, by criticizing you internally, a voice keeps you from doing what would be punished or criticized by someone else if you did it externally, protecting you from external criticism. This is sometimes called conscience, which is often depicted as an angel speaking into someone's ear.
2. The positive intent is to ally with the person criticizing you, in order to preserve an important relationship. For instance, a child will criticize himself in order to join with—and avoid separation from—a parent or other important caregiver. For a very small and helpless child, separation is equivalent to abandonment and death, so she or he will make great efforts to maintain connection with the parent or other caregiver, even when the parent is abusive or it means giving up other important personal needs. This is sometimes called "introjection," identifying with a powerful person and taking on his or her behavior, a dynamic that often occurs in response to abusive parents.
3. The positive intent is to improve your behavior or performance. A voice may criticize your shortcomings in an effort to improve what you do—just as your parents did in the past. The voice uses the parent's way of speaking, pointing out errors and mistakes, without giving positive guidance about how to do better. It doesn't have the skills to express caring in a more positive way.

C. The voice may have no intent. Very rarely a voice may respond that it doesn't have any positive (or negative) intent, or that it doesn't know what it is, or that it once had a positive intent but has forgotten what it was. It is even possible that the voice is just a random memory of what someone said to you at some time in the past, and you somehow thought that it applied to you, so there really isn't any positive intent. Since there is no positive intent, there is no reason for it to continue to say what it has been saying, so you can say, "OK, if you have no positive intent in saying this, would it be OK to stop saying that to me?"

> The only problem with this is that the voice now has nothing to do. Remember that every voice is an echo of a real person and situation, and people don't like to be idle; they like to have something to do. Without a positive alternative, the voice is likely to fall back into the only thing it knows. So it works better to ask, "Would you like to have a positive intent?" Assuming that it says yes, you can ask it to pick one, and it can help if you offer an example or two. "Would you like to have the positive intent of giving me complimentary feedback in order to support me at appropriate times, such as saying, 'Hey, you did that really well,' or 'You really took her feelings into account when you responded to her,' or something like that?"

A voice may have any, or several, or even all, of the different kinds of intent described above. If you review these different possibilities, you can realize why it is so useful to go through the process of retrieving and clarifying information, as discussed in Chapter 2. After gathering all that information, it often becomes obvious what the positive intent is, and you may not even have to ask for it. Although you may initially discover only one kind of positive intent, all these different kinds could be present simultaneously, and it can be useful to ask questions to find out more about them. When you think it could be useful to elicit an additional kind of positive intent, you can continue to ask until you discover it. You might say, "OK, your positive intent for me is that you want me to become more capable. What is your positive intent for yourself, or for my sister, or for someone else in my family, or even for a stranger?" When you can elicit two or more positive intents, that results in a broader and deeper understanding, and the change in your response to the voice will usually be more significant and lasting.

When you can identify the kinds of positive intent that an inner voice has, that gives you good information about what, if anything, needs to be done. For instance, if the intent was only for the voice, then nothing further needs to be done, because what the voice says really has nothing to do with you. It is just a background noise with no relevance to you—like the sound of wind, or raindrops on the roof. When you realize that the voice is not really talking about you, there is no need to have any response to it. Then it can be useful to give the voice something useful to do (see Chapter 6).

However, if the positive intent is to ally with a parent or other caregiver, then it may be very important to make some changes in your relationship with the voice. Simply agreeing with the positive intent is a first step, but it's usually useful to go beyond that. One possibility would be to differentiate between friendship and slavery, and to realize that acknowledging a parent's concerns doesn't require total obedience to his or her wishes, many of which may not be appropriate for you. Another possibility would be to use the forgiveness process (S. Andreas, 2000) to resolve any remaining resentment or anger you feel toward a parent.

If the voice's positive intent is to protect you from criticism, or to improve your abilities, then it will be important to explore how the voice can learn to speak more supportively, in order to better carry out its positive intent (see Chapter 7).

In the fall of 2006 I presented a conference workshop titled "Transforming Troublesome Internal Voices" (Andreas, 2006b). Near the end of the workshop, I invited a participant who had discovered the positive intent of her critical voice to speak to the group. The transcript below is essentially verbatim, edited only slightly for clarity.

Addie: Before break, we were talking about the positive intent of this critical voice. And I am almost 5 years in recovery from an eating disorder. And so those voices have plagued me since I was probably 8 . . . so a really long time. And I was sitting back there, and I could not for the life of me figure out any kind of positive intent of these voices. Because they almost destroyed me. They were cruel. And I have worked and worked, and I was just back there struggling, and I came and asked you [Steve] at break. And you said there was a positive intent.

Steve: Well, I assume that.

Addie: Yes, that there was probably a positive intent. And you encouraged me to go back and work with my friend Luke back there—the guy in the blue. Raise your hand.

Steve: Raise your hand. Take some credit. This is a time when you can go like this. (Steve reaches around and pats himself on the back.)

Addie: Wonderful. And then you [Steve] offered, if I wanted to, if there was time, later, to work with you if I was willing. So I went back and did the exercise that we all did, with Luke. And something occurred to me that I've never—and I've been in therapy, you know, weekly and biweekly, since being in recovery, so it's been something that I've worked on with a therapist and a nutritionist. And both of those specialize in eating disorders, and out of 5 years, and thousands of dollars worth of therapy, I had never thought about it in this way.

Through that exercise I realized that the positive intent was for me to feel good about myself. Now the delivery of that message sucked, because it came through words like, "You're ugly." "You're fat," you know, "Don't eat that." You know. "You've eaten too much—no one will like you." "You're not good enough." "You're not pretty enough. You're not—" You know. I mean just devastatingly cruel.

So, like I said, through that exercise, I realized that what that voice was trying to help me do was to feel good about the person that I am. And so I worked with Luke back there in reframing, and then I asked that voice, instead of telling me I'm lazy because I didn't get my fat ass to the gym, to tell me to rest my body—that if you're tired, you must need rest. And that helped.

And instead of focusing on my outside to assure me that people will see the beauty, you know, within, you know, instead of "You've gotta weigh this, and wear this size for people to like you," I asked the voice to say, "Please, they'll like you—see your beauty within." You know, "Be yourself. Show people who you are, let them see your heart." And, um—it was really kind of overwhelming, and I'm getting ready to start to cry, so I apologize if I do.

Steve: No, you don't need to apologize. And—tears—there are many kinds of tears. Let me do a mini-lecture for a minute. And you [Addie] tell me if I get something wrong. There are tears of sorrow. Right? Somebody leaves; somebody dies. There are tears of reunion; a soldier comes back from the war, you cry. There are tears of relief; if you are in great pain for a long time and somebody gives you a shot of some good stuff—"Ahhh," there's tears of relief. Tears of reunion are very beautiful, and I think that's what you're feeling. Does that make sense to you?

Addie: Yeah.

Steve: Tears of reunion, getting back in touch with something—of becoming whole again.

Addie: Freedom.

Steve: Freedom.

Addie: Freedom.

Steve: So maybe there's some relief, too?

Addie: Yes.

Steve: So they can be mixed. You can have a mixture of tears. And the reunion kind of tears have been described by a mystic friend of mine as "tears of truth." And my tears of truth might be different than yours, or somebody else's, but somehow they are very true for me, and I think you're getting a touch of that kind of thing—is that right? (Addie nods.)

And I recommend that you cultivate this experience. You know, some people cultivate grudges. They collect horrible memories, and so on like that. (In transactional analysis, they call this gunnysacking—collect all your resentments in a gunnysack, and then periodically dumping them all on somebody.) This (tears of truth) has been described to me by my mystic friend [Van Dusen, 1996] who is now dead—and I hope he has found what he expected—but anyway, that if you follow your tears of truth—the times when you are deeply touched by some kind of courage (Steve's voice starts to break) or exceptional—see, I've been collecting for years, so it's easy for me to bring these up and hard to talk about them. But that these kinds of tears of truth—they are to be cultivated and honored, and can lead you to live a life that is very, very rich and wonderful. So I would encourage you to honor those tears fully. Sound good?

Addie: (softly) It does.

Steve: OK. Is there anything you [participants] would like to ask her? I think she's been very eloquent, so, thanks very much. (Applause from the audience.)

Woman: I was just wondering, Addie, if you get a sense that you're going to be able to integrate this work, and that it wasn't just a fleeting experience that you had here, but that this is something that is going to remain with you. Was it that kind of powerful work? Or was it an emotional experience for you?

Addie: It was both.

Steve: (to Addie) She wants you to make a prediction.

Addie: I predict, and actually part of that exercise was to ask the voice if it would do this—if it would take on this positive role instead of, you know, just destroying me. And I think, and what I came up with, is that it's going to take time, because I'm 32 years old, and these voices have been with me for 25 years in the way that they are—the cruel, the mean, you know, and I've spent the last 5 years trying to push them away and make them stop, but they've always been there. And it's always been there in the negative way.

So I think it's going to take some time, and I think I'm going to have to remind that voice what it promised. And when we were working with the exercise, and I did that, that was the feeling that I got that this voice, this—I've named my—I call it my diseased eating disorder—I named it Eunice. And if anybody has a Eunice that they love, I'm really sorry. But Eunice, this entity, this thing, would be willing to speak positively, but would need my help in reminding it.

Steve: OK. (To the audience member) Now, you're talking to her conscious mind now. (To Addie) I want to talk to your unconscious mind. (Softly) Ask that voice—Eunice?

Addie: Eunice, yeah.

Steve: Close your eyes. Ask her if she needs any reminder.

Addie: (softly) Yes, she does.

Steve: She does. OK. How often?

Addie: I don't think she knows.

Steve: Ask her anyway. If she did know, what would she say? Or let me offer this—what I'm suggesting is that you make a deal with her to remind her a certain number of times a day, and I would like to know how often she would like to be reminded so that you could do that. And maybe as a start, maybe more than Eunice thinks would be absolutely necessary, but plenty, and then you could try reducing it periodically, and explore this a little bit. But if she does need to be reminded, then it's important that you do remind her.

Addie: At this point I can't tell whether it's my fear or her fear.

Steve: Yeah.

Addie: I can't tell which is coming out, because what I'm feeling from her is that initially, in the beginning, she'll need reminding every time.

Steve: Yeah. How often is that?

Addie: Oh, well, some days it's hundreds. Other days, it's just a couple.

Steve: And do you know when it would be appropriate to remind her? Do you know what kind of cues are the kinds of things—or are you saying that she might just come out and say the old stuff again, and you just need to remind her?

Addie: Yeah.

Steve: Oh, great. Then you just wait until this voice—

Addie: As it comes out.

Steve: Now I have a hunch she's wrong.

Addie: Really?

Steve: I have a hunch that you don't need to do anything else. But I could be wrong. So—(joking) I've been wrong once before (laughter).

Addie: You were right about the positive intent.

Steve: Yes, I was right about that. And the experience you had back there, of that relief and that warmth, and I forget exactly how you described it. (Softly) Close your eyes for a moment, and memorize that experience. Often we don't take the time to really savor an experience—even though it may be wonderful at the time—and really savor it and remember it, so that it becomes a resource that you can count on. . . .

Got it? That looks great. (Softly) Now I want you to do one more thing before you open your eyes. Allow that feeling to go throughout your whole body—out to your fingertips, even your fingernails, up to the top of your head, down to your toes, down to your toenails, so that every cell in your body can remember that experience of integration. . . .

And that Eunice can do the same. That she can have that go right out to her fingertips, right down to her toes, out to her ears, out to the top of her head, out to the surface of her skin so that she can remember that fully and automatically whenever it's appropriate—whenever she wants to remind you to pay attention to your own needs and your own values, to feel good about yourself from the inside. . . .

Now you take as long as you want to do that. It's time for the session to be over, and if you want to—I don't know if you're going to another session, to the keynote or anything—oh, we have lunch. Anyway, take the time, whatever time you need, to be by yourself, and not suddenly be talking to people, and just take a bath in that—like a bubble bath or a sauna or something like that—and really just feel that throughout your whole body.

Addie: I feel light!

Steve: Yeah. Thanks very much (applause).

Follow-Up

Immediately after the workshop I talked to Addie some more, and found that throughout college she was a binge drinker before the eating disorder, which was binging and purging. I asked her what she thought would have happened if she had known about this positive intent when she was younger. She was very thoughtful for a while, and then said, "I think I wouldn't have had to go through any of that."

I e-mailed Addie a little over 2 years after the workshop, asking if I should use her real name, and if it was OK to include the comment in the previous paragraph that she made to me after the workshop. Here is her reply:

> Absolutely use my real name and the comment that was not on the workshop CD. That experience with you changed my life, and I would be honored for other people to read about it! I must tell you that reading my experience on paper came not one minute too soon. I've been struggling with Eunice's particularly loud and critical voice for the last few months. Reading the transcript took me immediately back to that day and those moments of truth. I could actually feel the emotion and power all over again and was reminded of Eunice's promise. Now I must remind her. Thank you, Steve, for your guidance and for what you helped me to do for myself that day. Even though I'm struggling somewhat with the critical voice, I am still very happy and doing very well. (personal communication, 2008)

I contacted Addie again in 2013, and asked her if she had anything to report after 7 years. This is what she wrote:

> Thank you for contacting me—it's been great to revisit my whole experience and get in touch with it in a way I haven't in a long time. I also want to thank you from the bottom of my heart for working with me seven years ago—I don't have adequate words to describe how much it has meant to my life!
>
> It was uncanny timing that you called me in November, 2013. A few days prior to your call, I was cleaning out some file cabinets and found the transcript of our conversation during your break-out session, "Transforming Troublesome

Voices." It had been many years since I'd read it and rereading it took me back to that day as well as my moment of realization and processing it with you (in front of what seemed like one thousand strangers). The surge of emotion and memories made me cry.

Reading the transcript followed by your phone call a few days later couldn't have come at a better time. I've been struggling with Eunice (the name I gave my troublesome voice). Over the past eight months or so, I've been under a considerable amount of stress. Historically, when I have felt out of control of outside circumstances, I have turned to "controlling" food and my weight. After our work together, I understand that Eunice is trying to help me reduce stress by "encouraging" me to control what I can. According to her, all is right with the world if I'm thin, pretty and physically fit.

However, her delivery sucks, and she and I have been having a battle of the wills as to how she will reframe it and what I need/don't need to hear from her. She's stubborn and I have days when her intrusive words are loud, especially after gaining six pounds since getting married last February. To Eunice (me) that might as well be 20 pounds.

I continue to remind her, and myself, of her promise to not motivate by criticism and to be gentle with her words. Although sometimes I continue to struggle, I'm able to pull on the work done at the conference and no longer feel like a prisoner in my own mind. In order to regularly check out my own thinking, I have a therapist and psychiatrist with whom I work, as well as an incredible support system!

My husband doesn't understand my body image and food issues, but is reassuring, loving, and validates my feelings. To make me laugh he always says, "Baby doll, I still think you need to eat a buttermilk biscuit!" He's an answer to my prayers!

I'm so grateful that I'm able to bring what I learned into my clinical practice. My patient population typically consists of individuals with mood disorders, chemical dependency, personality disorders and mild (if there is such a thing) levels of psychosis. Most, if not all, have spent a majority of their lives struggling with the messages from troublesome internal voices. I use what I learned those years ago to present the perspective that there is a benign intent underneath the malicious words. Not all have had the insight and self-awareness to fully grasp the concept (some look at me as if I've grown another head), but there are times when I have seen "light bulbs." I work with an acute population and in a short-term program, so there's not much time to go further. However, I am grateful to have been able to plant a seed and to spread what was planted for me! Thank you for everything Steve!

—Addie

Next I want to demonstrate how to use what I have presented so far to help someone change an internal voice by presenting a transcript of an actual session, without knowing anything about the content. This completely respects people's privacy, since they don't have to talk about any of the difficult and possibly embarrassing experiences they have had. It also makes the process much faster and easier, and it makes it much easier to attend to and learn the steps of the process, since you won't be distracted by the content.

4. Putting It Together

In Chapters 1 through 3 I have discussed the usefulness of three related processes: (1) joining with a voice in order to create a friendly alliance with it; (2) retrieving and clarifying information; and (3) discovering the positive intent of a voice. Each of these three processes are useful in themselves, and since they all support each other, they could be used in any order. However, they are most useful if they are used in the order I have presented. If you haven't already joined and allied with a voice, it may not be willing to offer you much information. And if you haven't already retrieved information, the positive intent may be puzzling and difficult to understand fully.

The verbatim transcript below illustrates how to use this sequence with someone else, and is followed by an outline of the steps so that you can use it for working with your own troublesome internal voice. The transcript was made from an audio recording of a presentation on working with belief systems at a Milton H. Erickson Foundation Brief Therapy Conference. (Andreas & Dilts, 2008). This conference included a wide variety of presentations related to the work of Milton H. Erickson, who was probably the most innovative and effective therapist who ever lived. Rather than just talking about how to work with a belief system, I asked for a volunteer for a live demonstration.

Steve: What I would like to have is someone up here who has a troublesome voice. It could be a critical voice; it could be one that forecasts horrible futures or anything like that, but something that bugs you a bunch of times. And in a sense this is a belief, because if you didn't believe in this voice, it wouldn't be a problem, right? I mean, every once in a while have you had someone say to you something really off the wall and you just think, "Well, I guess they're schizophrenic or something—it doesn't have anything to do with me."

So if you listen to a troublesome voice and if you're troubled by it, then it means you believe it, right? So there's one little piece, and I'd like to show you one way of working with beliefs. There are lots and lots of ways. So who would be interested? (A woman raises her hand.) OK, good. And you are?

Lynne: Lynne.

Steve: Lynne. OK, great. You get to hold the "rock star" (handheld) mike. OK. And I'm going to do this content free, by the way. And a lot of the forms of reframing require that you know some content, but this is a way of doing reframing without any content at all. OK? Is that OK with you?

Lynne: If you can do it.

Steve: (confidently) Oh, yeah, I can do it (laughter).

Lynne: OK.

Steve: OK, so you hear a voice, right?

Lynne: I do.

Steve: Can you hear it right now?

Lynne: Mmhm.

Steve: Great. Do you know whose voice this is?

Lynne: Mmhm.

Steve: Great. Now I want you to listen to the tonality of the voice for starters. It's probably unpleasant, so I won't have you do this too long, but just close your eyes and listen to the tonality, and the details, the hesitations, the emphasis, the verbal emphasis, what part is loud, what part is soft, and so on, as it speaks to you. . . . OK? And you know who it is, right? Can you see their face? (Lynne sighs.) You know who it is, so I want you to see their face as they say these words to you.

Lynne: Can I comment?

Steve: Sure, sure. Anytime. Give me feedback anytime—all the time.

Lynne: A little content. This happened a very long time ago.

Steve: That's fine, but I don't want the content.

Lynne: No, I wasn't going to tell you, but—so I remember the impact of it better than I remember the actual words.

Steve: Right, you remember the impact, the emotional impact.

Lynne: And I'm still carrying the impact.

Steve: Exactly, and that's what we want to change. Now in order to change that, I need you to do some other things.

Lynne: OK.

Steve: OK? So close your eyes and do your best to visualize this person. It doesn't have to be totally clear. People have freak-out phobias with very, very dull, dim images. You don't have to have a crystal-clear positive hallucination or anything.

Lynne: OK.

Steve: Can you see the person's face as they say this to you?

Lynne: Yeah.

Steve: Can you see it now?

Lynne: Yes.

Steve: When you see this person's face, does it make any difference in your understanding of the meaning of the words? It may or may not.

Lynne: Not much.

Steve: You say "not much." Does that mean it's a little different . . . or the same? (Lynne is near tears.) It's really getting to you, isn't it? OK. We'll change this real fast. So take a little break. And I want you to see the larger context around this interaction. Can you see that? So there is this person speaking to you. Where are they speaking to you? And again I don't want to know the answer, but I want you to visualize the larger context. . . .

Lynne: Mmhm.

Steve: Now, when you see the larger context, does that change the meaning? Again, it might or it might not.

Lynne: (in a more lively voice) I think it did.

Steve: OK. And we can explore that later. I just want you to notice. So the larger context made a difference, right?

Lynne: Yeah.

Steve: OK. You look like it's more comfortable now.

Lynne: Yeah.

Steve: OK. Great. Actually, give me a little bit of a report. Without revealing content, just how is it different seeing the whole context?

Lynne: I like the place.

Steve: You like the place. OK. So the place is comfortable, or pretty, or—you like it in some way.

Lynne: Mmhm.

Steve: OK. Great. Now I want you to expand the context in another way. What happened just before this event?

Lynne: I don't actually know.

Steve: Well, hallucinate it then. Make it up. What do you think happened just before this, in the few minutes or the half hour before this event? . . . And also what happened after? Expand your sense of this event in time, both before and after. And let me know when you've done that. . . .

Lynne: I can't do before.

Steve: You can't do before. OK. You can't even imagine what might have happened before?

Lynne: Well—

Steve: What if you just made it up? What do you think might have happened?

Lynne: Umhmn.

Steve: Does that change it at all?

Lynne: (taking a deep breath) Well, in the sense that we shifted away from the event.

Steve: OK. Good. (To the audience) So, can you hear her? Some no and some yes. (To Lynne) I know it's a chore [to hold up the microphone]. But if you can—say again what you said—something about shifting the attention away from the—

Lynne: It shifts the attention away from the actual event. It just lightens it.

Steve: So it lightens it, right. This is called "perspective," seeing something in a larger context, and often it shifts the meaning. At least it makes the emotional impact different, even if it doesn't shift the meaning. OK? Now, you know this person, is that right?

Lynne: Mmm.

Steve: Very well?

Lynne: Mmm.

Steve: OK. Now I want you to contemplate their strengths, their limitations, who they are as a person, their history, all the background that this comment came out of. They said something to you. And initially we started with just the voice, and then we added in all these other things, and now I'm asking you to add in your knowledge of this person and their limitations and their difficulties, their history, their hopes, their desires—anything you know about this person (long pause). . . .

Lynne: Do you want feedback?

Steve: Yeah, a little bit. Again, not content, but just if it shifts your experience, I would be interested in some little report.

Lynne: (softly) I'm feeling sorry for them.

Steve: "Feeling sorry for them." Oh, that's a very different feeling than you had just a little while ago, is that right?

Lynne: Mmhm.

Steve: Before it was feeling somehow diminished or terrorized, or something—I don't know what, right? And now you are feeling sorry for them.

Lynne: Mmhm.

Steve: Great. That's a very useful change, I think. Now I want you to do one more—well, several more things, but the next thing—I'm going to give you a whole bunch of good stuff here. Ask that voice—ask that person—"If you could tell me fully what you meant to say by what you said, including the background—your feelings, the experience that this statement came out of, what would you say?" And just listen for her response, or his response. . . . (Lynne is showing strong feelings.) I can tell that's very powerful for you. I don't know the details. Is it useful? Can you tell me? . . . (Lynne takes a deep breath.) "Are you learning something?" is another way of saying it.

Lynne: I think so.

Steve: Yes? Do you want to do that a little more, or do you want to go on? . . . We can always come back later, of course. (Lynne laughs.) It's your brain, and you're stuck with it.

Lynne: (laughing) OK.

Steve: OK? So it told you—it clarified the message in some way?

Lynne: More information. (Lynne begins to have some soft tears.)

Steve: More information, yeah—a larger background?

Lynne: Yes.

Steve: Does anybody have any Kleenex? In the front row here? Well, here (offering), this is a relatively clean handkerchief.

Lynne: (laughing) It will probably get makeup all over it.

Steve: I don't care about that. (Someone in the front row offers some tissues.) OK, now we're all set.

Lynne: (to the person who provided tissues) Thank you.

Steve: Thank you. OK. So this person told you in greater detail the—ah, you have more of a basis to understand what this person said, is that right?

Lynne: Yes.

Steve: Great. Close your eyes. (Lynne takes a deep breath.) And thank this person (Lynne laughs) for the clarification. It might sound silly.

Lynne: No, it wasn't that. It wasn't that it was silly.

Steve: OK. All right. (Lynne takes several deep breaths.) . . . You're getting quite a few changes out of this. (Lynne laughs.) And you let me know if there's any time that there is some kind of problem, or . . . I'm sure this is useful; I've done this a bunch.

Lynne: Yeah.

Steve: OK. The next thing I want you to do is ask that person for their positive intent when they spoke to you in that way. What was their positive intent? It could be a very limited positive intent coming out of their own frustration—they just needed to yell at somebody at that moment. It could have been that they were worried about you, and they spoke out of their worry, and they were not very good at communicating, so they said it in a crummy way that made you feel bad all these years. And ask them for their positive intent. And then listen to what they say back.

Lynne: I'm not sure how much information I can give you.

Steve: That's all right.

Lynne: They were mostly defending someone else.

Steve: OK. So they were trying to protect somebody else?

Lynne: It wasn't about hurting me.

Steve: What was that?

Lynne: It wasn't about hurting me.

Steve: It wasn't about hurting you, yeah. Good. OK, great. And, again, thank them for that—for their communication. (There is a long pause, while Lynne repeatedly breathes deeply.) . . . That's pretty different now, isn't it?

Lynne: They're sorry. . . .

Steve: Yeah, they're sorry. Oh, good. Do you have any questions about this? . . . Would it be OK if people asked you questions, as long as you have total freedom to not answer anything they ask?

Lynne: Yes!

Steve: OK. There's a mike there if anybody would like to ask her questions. Please sort out your questions between her and me. You know, questions for me about the method, or what I'm doing or what's going on—theory stuff. And her—it's just about her experience. If you have any questions for her, let's have those first. . . .

Man in audience: Steve, after you do this kind of work—

Steve: Wait, you're asking me? First, any questions for her, and then we can let her rest.

Man: OK, the question for you [Lynne] is the same. Now that you've done the work, what's the affective response to the event that occurred to you a long time ago?

Lynne: I'm sorry. I didn't hear you; can you ask louder?

Man: You worked through a belief system based on an event. The question is, what is your emotional, affective—

Steve: (translating) How do you feel now? (Lynne laughs.) How's that?

Lynne: Thank you.

Man: Thank you.

Steve: These psychiatrist types can go on forever! (The audience laughs; Lynne laughs, and the man asking the question chuckles.)

Man: How do you feel about what happened to you when you were little, right now? What are you feeling now?

Lynne: Better, better.

Man: What does "better" mean?

Lynne: Yeah. A little relieved. A little relieved. It's interesting because I didn't get any information I didn't have before, but there was something different about the way I got it—I'm not sure that answers the question.

(Throughout the process, Lynne's nonverbal behavior—tears, sighing, facial expression, relaxation, smiling, and so on—was eloquent in demonstrating the various changes that she was going through, and how much better she was feeling at the end. I wish that I had said something at the time to point out that to attach specific words to these changes was not really necessary.)

Steve: Any other questions for her? Use the mike. Well, go ahead.

Woman in audience: Was it hard to thank the person?

Steve: (repeating) Was it hard to thank the person?

Lynne: (firmly) No. No.

Steve: Very congruent answer, right? One more question for her and then—

Second woman in audience: I may have missed this in the beginning, but what was your belief, and how has that changed?

Steve: We don't know, because I wanted to do this without content.

Woman 2: Without the content—

Steve: All I know is there was some kind of voice that terrorized her or made her feel terrible at the beginning.

Woman 2: OK. But the belief you had has changed?

Steve: Ask her.

Lynne: Yeah (taking a deep breath). . . .

(Again, the question asks for the content of the belief, and a request for a verbal confirmation that she has changed, when her nonverbal behavior was already eloquent.)

Steve: Let me ask her—here's a better way to do it. Lynne, can you hear the original voice now? . . .

Lynne: I don't feel the way I felt.

Steve: Right. You can still hear the original voice, but you feel differently.

Lynne: But I feel differently.

Steve: Right.

Lynne: Yes.

Steve: That's a real concrete specific thing. If you talk too much about words and beliefs you can get a little lost, but she feels different and she feels more ah, whole, more settled, more—

Lynne: Freer.

Steve: Freer. Yeah. That's really the answer. OK, thanks very much.

Lynne: Thank you (audience applause).

(The demonstration and commentary above took 10 minutes.)

Now let me just say a couple of words about this. Beliefs are not just words. Beliefs are generalizations that are usually based on concrete, very specific experiences. If you stay with the words, you can get really lost, and you can wander around in the swamp forever. If you have a specific example—this is called a prototype in cognitive linguistics (Lakoff, 1987)—then you work with that. All I did here was repeatedly increase the scope of what Lynne was experiencing, in both space and time, what is often described as "seeing the big picture." Initially she just has a set of words. You get the face, the person, the background of the person, the context. I kept expanding the scope of her experience, and when you do that, the meaning typically changes, sometimes radically.

Just one very simple example, and then I'll stop. One woman had two sisters who belittled her all the time, and so she had these voices of her sisters yammering at her all the time. All she did—when she saw the sisters' faces, she realized they were jealous. The belittling had nothing to do with her. It had to do with their feeling bad, their feeling diminished, and the only way they could deal with that was to defensively belittle her. That totally changed the meaning of the whole thing, and her response was completely different. Usually it changes all along, or sometimes one thing doesn't make a difference but another thing does, but there's a whole series of things that you can do.

But basically, you start with the voice, whose voice is it, you add the face, you get the context—the immediate context, the larger context, the time context—what happened before, what's happening after—and then you go for the background—who is this person, what is their positive intent, what lifestyle is this coming out of, what is their stance in life, blah, blah, blah. But it's a concrete, specific experience, and that's what makes it work.

Lynne said, "I didn't get any information I didn't have before, but there was something different about the way I got it," and I'd like to say a bit about my understanding of how this was different, and why it got a more useful response:

1. We took a specific, concrete experience and worked with that, rather than with an abstract generalization or a set of words that is only a tiny sound bite from that experience.
2. Using pure process instructions, I asked her to attend to many different aspects of that experience that she had not been attending to, enlarging the context in both space and time.
3. As she enriched her understanding of the voice in many ways, she experienced all this together simultaneously—rather than separately, or sequentially.
4. By expanding her experience of the voice she could see the big picture, and she had a different response to this richer perspective.

Although a conference demonstration is a unique situation, the events in this transcript are typical of the sequence of changes that someone experiences as I offer a series of instructions that are completely content free. This is quite different from most therapies, which are usually focused on content, and are often meandering, and don't produce dependable results. After each intervention, I asked Lynne to report any changes. After some of the interventions she experienced little or no change, but with others she had major changes.

Since I had no idea what her internal voice was saying to her, there was no possibility that she could be embarrassed by revealing any sensitive personal information. Working without content also makes it impossible for me to influence her experience—either verbally or nonverbally—with my values or opinions about the content.

After each intervention, I carefully observed her nonverbal responses to make my own assessment of any changes, comparing what I saw and heard in the moment with her initial state, or her state immediately preceding the intervention. This provided me with immediate feedback, so that I could adjust what I did to be sure that I was communicating effectively, and that she was succeeding in doing what I asked her to. In contrast, feedback at the end of a session—or much later—is always much more global, and doesn't permit the kind of adjustments that I made to her responses in the moment.

At the end of this session, Lynne realized that the words that had troubled her were intended to protect someone else, and were not intended to hurt her. Lynne was sorry for the person whose voice had been making her feel bad for so many years, and the voice was sorry about it, too. The voice is now a cooperative ally, speaking to her as a friend, and they are no longer opponents in conflict.

Five years after my session with Lynne, I contacted her by email and she sent me the following written report:

> I have made major changes in my life, and although I don't credit the work I did with you completely, I do think it was a significant piece. The voice I heard was my mother telling me to protect my sister's feelings by—and of course this was my interpretation—hiding my own gifts. So I created a very compartmentalized life in which I kept the secret of all the things I can do; people who knew me as a therapist didn't know I was also a singer/songwriter and vice-versa. When I recorded a CD I not only refused to have my picture on it, I forgot to put my name on the CD itself! So those who got the CD without the jacket wouldn't know who it was, and had no way to get in touch with me.
>
> Three years ago I agreed to host an Internet radio show (thelynneshow.com)—more public, but still not visible. Then I began writing a one-woman musical piece; I didn't understand until it was almost finished that it was a challenge to this lifelong taboo. I produced and performed *Under the Radar* last year, on my 70th birthday. It was the most terrifying thing I'd ever done—until I played the video for my family, including my sister.

5. Listening for an Underlying Problem

The verbatim transcript below provides another example of working with a troublesome voice by joining with it, retrieving and clarifying information, and determining its positive intent. By now you may be thinking, "Why so many transcripts?" Since each client is different, the same process needs to be adapted to each client's individual needs. A transcript shows exactly what I have said to a client, and exactly how the client responded. This is vitally important information which is usually omitted in most discussions of methods of therapy. Most writing about therapy talks about goals, like, "gain rapport" or "establish a safe space," etc., with nothing about what to say or do to actually accomplish that. Since this transcript is from a video, rather than an audio recording, I have been able to add descriptions of our nonverbal gestures, because they are so important in the two-way communication between us. Pamela's gestures amplify and confirm what she is communicating about her experience, and mine express my understanding of her experience, and also clarify exactly what changes I'm asking her to make.

In the course of using this process with Pamela, it becomes evident that the voice is depressing her. The voice she hears is that of a special person who has died, and Pamela is still grieving this loss, sometimes thinking, "It's better to die, and to get it over it with; death is better than feeling the sadness." I offer her a process for resolving grief (Andreas & Andreas, 2002) that goes far beyond most grief work in which a client only expresses grief, but is still left with the empty feelings of loss. The grief resolution process reconnects Pamela with the person who has died, and the positive feelings she had with that person. It does this by asking her to vividly remember the dead person, seeing, hearing, touching, and even smelling and tasting him.

The transcript was made from a video recording of a clinical demonstration titled "Transforming Negative Self-Talk—Devils Into Angels," at the Milton H. Erickson Foundation Brief Therapy Conference in December 2012. I began by asking for a volunteer for the demonstration.

Steve: I want to tell you the basis on which you volunteer. You have a troublesome internal voice, a critical internal voice, or one that gets you down somehow, or that you don't like, and you're willing to tell me the content of the voice only. You don't have to tell me anything else. I won't be going back in your history and so on. Other than that, it will be content free. (Pamela volunteers; I see from her name tag that she is from South America, but her English is very fluent.)

Steve: OK, so, Pamela, you have a voice?

Pamela: Yeah.

Steve: Tell me what it says.

Pamela: I have a voice that says that, "Even though I have achieved many things, nothing makes sense."

Steve: "Even though—?" Tell me again.

Pamela: "Even though I have many things going—many things going for me, . . . nothing makes sense."

Steve: OK. "Even though I've got many things going for me, nothing makes sense."

In retrospect, I wish I had asked her to try a very simple sequence reversal that can make a profound difference in experience: "Now I want you to say the same words in a different order: 'Even though nothing makes sense, I've got many things going for me.'" If you try out this reversal, you can easily verify that the words that immediately follow "Even though" tend to be ignored, while the words after the comma tend to be emphasized and experienced more fully. A smaller intervention would be to reverse the sequence while giving the two parts of the sentence equal emphasis by using "and" in place of "even though": "Nothing makes sense and I've got many things going for me." Or I could have asked her to substitute "and" in the original sequence: "I've got many things going for me, and nothing makes sense." Each of these interventions will change what she attends to, and what she emphasizes, somewhat differently.

Steve: Now, where do you hear this voice? (I begin by asking about the location of the voice, because once I know that, I can suggest changes in location that are likely to change Pamela's response to it in useful ways.

Pamela: Where in my body?

Steve: Umhm. Or where in your personal space? (Pamela gestures to her forehead, and Steve gestures to his forehead. Nonverbal gestures are a very important part of communication. By copying her gesture, I am unambiguously confirming my understanding nonverbally. Even more important, I am nonverbally putting myself into her experience—the basis for empathy and understanding—and I do this throughout the session. In contrast, if I had pointed to her forehead, that would have conveyed a more distant and objective understanding.) Right up here?

Pamela: Umhm.

Steve: OK, great. ("OK, great" is a simple acceptance of her experience, and you will notice these or similar words frequently in this transcript.)

Pamela: And sometimes here (gesturing toward her heart area).

Steve: Also here? (Steve gestures to his heart area.)

Pamela: Yeah.

Steve: Now, you hear it down here?

Pamela: Yeah, here.

Steve: You actually hear it down there. That's a very bad choice. (Audience laughter. By using the word "choice" I presuppose that Pamela was active in choosing this arrangement and, more important, it presupposes that she can choose differently.)

Pamela: Hmm.

Steve: I don't know how you got there, but that's a bad choice. (Audience laughter) How about taking the voice that's down here (gesturing to his heart area) and moving it up to join the voice that's up here (gesturing to his forehead). It's the same voice, right?

Pamela: (nodding) Yes.

Steve: OK. Just try that, move it up here (gesturing from his heart area up to his forehead with his right hand; Pamela does the same with her right hand. This is a nice confirmation that she is actually doing what I asked her to do. This is the first of many specific instructions to change some aspect of her internal world, in order to find out how her feeling experience changes in response. Although I have some ideas about what kind of change may be useful, I am always guided by her immediate report and response to a suggested change.) Good, it can be helpful to use your hand.

Pamela: OK (nodding). Umhm.

Steve: Now, when it's all up here in your forehead—is it outside your forehead or inside?

Pamela: Inside.

Steve: Inside?

Pamela: Umhm.

Steve: OK, and it's all together there inside?

Pamela: I have it here (gesturing to her forehead) and here (gesturing to her heart area).

Steve: Yeah. But have you got it all moved up now? Sounds to me like maybe some is still down there (gesturing to her heart area).

Pamela: Hmm. Yeah.

Steve: OK. Move it all up.

Pamela: Hmm, OK.

Steve: You can hear it clearer. Part of your confusion is that you're hearing two things from two different spaces.

Pamela: Yeah, umhm.

Steve: Right?

Pamela: Umhm.

Steve: So when it's all together you'll be able to hear it better. And we'll change that.

Pamela: OK.

Steve: But first you need to put them together, I think.

Pamela: (nodding) OK.

Steve: Got it?

Pamela: Umhm.

Steve: Now, when it's all up here, close your eyes, and listen to that voice. Do you have a different response to it now?

Pamela: Hmm.

Steve: Is there any difference in response?

Pamela: Umm—

Steve: Sometimes it'll be different; sometimes it won't.

Pamela: It's so lapidating. (Pamela's right hand gestures in a pushing-down movement, a suggestion of depression. I had never heard this word before, so I had no idea what she meant. Later I found that it means "to pelt with stones, to stone to death," which is even more depressing than I realized at the time. However, notice that I never use the word "depression," which is a kind of catchall term for a wide variety of experiences. Instead I simply focus on her internal experience.)

Steve: What is that?

Pamela: Lapidating. You know, like—(Pamela gestures in a pushing-down movement with her right hand. This is another hint that the voice is depressing her—"depress" means to push down.)

Steve: Pushing you down?

Pamela: Umhm.

Steve: Yeah, but is it different than it was in your chest?

Pamela: Yeah.

Steve: OK, can you say how it's different?

Pamela: It's less oppressive.

Steve: Less oppressive, great. Now that's a nice change, right?

Pamela: Hmm.

Steve: (to the audience) Change does not have to take long. Change can be very quick. You may need a lot of little quick changes to get to an eventual outcome, but I believe that all change is almost instantaneous. When you make that little shift like this, it makes a difference.

Pamela: Umhm.

Steve: Now, which way does the voice point? Like my voice is pointing to you right now (gesturing from his mouth toward Pamela) and yours to me (gesturing from Pamela to himself). And the voice up here, which way it is pointing? (Pamela gestures from her forehead down toward her chest.) Down?

Pamela: Down.

Steve: Great. (Copying her gesture) Straight down?

Pamela: Straight down.

Steve: Straight down. No wonder it's pushing you down. (The direction of the voice is at least as important as its content in pushing her down and depressing her. To the audience)These things all make sense when you get down to the bottom of things. (To Pamela) Now, I want you to turn the voice around so it's pointing up. So what happens if you point it up?

Pamela: (nodding thoughtfully) Well, it's less oppressive.

Steve: It's better?

Pamela: It's better. Yeah.

Steve: Good. OK. Now, what if you put it up even further? Put that up about 4 or 5 feet.

(The audience comments that they can't hear; there is an interruption of several minutes while the sound system is adjusted.)

Steve: (to the audience) OK, so let's take off where we—pick up where we left off. So initially, just to summarize, she had this voice up and above her forehead—no, just inside her forehead—pointing down and she also had a voice here in her chest. Same voice, right? And first I moved this (gesturing toward his chest) to be with this (gesturing to his forehead) because having a nasty voice in your body is very, very bad and a lot of people do. And people sometimes have addictions and other compulsions to eat and stuff like that and it's because they have this voice in their stomach, and to have a critical voice in your stomach feels really, really bad. It's not good at all. So you—it's natural to try and eat and correct it and do something about it. It's—what do you call it—"self-medication" is the fancy term for it. OK. So just then I asked her to turn the voice around so that it's going up (to Pamela) and that made it lighter, right?

Pamela: Umhm.

Steve: (to the audience) And earlier, notice she said it pushes down—it pushed her down when it was pointing down. So now it's pointing up and now I just asked her to move it up about 4 feet, and I haven't gotten the report yet on that—I thought it would be good to summarize a little bit, since some of you had difficulty hearing.

Pamela: OK.

Steve: OK. So if you move it up about 5 feet?

Pamela: Five feet, it's like—how many meters? One meter? (Audience laughter.)

Steve: Oh, 2 meters.

Pamela: Two meters. OK.

Steve: Doesn't matter.

Pamela: It's better.

Steve: It's better?

Pamela: (nodding) Yes.

Steve: Now, when it's up there, can you hear it more clearly?

Pamela: No.

Steve: Not more clear? OK. So is it—do you still know what the words say?

Pamela: Ah, yes, but it's vague.

Steve: Vague, OK. So it feels better?

Pamela: (nodding) It feels better.

Steve: So you're—

Pamela: Less important.

Steve: I'm sorry?

Pamela: Less important.

Steve: Less important. Yeah, less impactful?

Pamela: Yeah.

Steve: Less emotional and impactful?

Pamela: Umhm.

Steve: Now that alone I think will help with your confusion. (Pamela nods.)

Pamela: Yeah.

Steve: Is that right?

Pamela: That's right. Yeah.

Steve: Now, I want you to listen to that voice, even though it's a little hard to hear and you can bring it down a little closer (gesturing from above his head down to his head) or you can make it a little louder if you want—

Pamela: OK.

Steve: —So that you can hear it more clearly.

Pamela: Umhm.

Steve: OK?

Pamela: Umhm.

Steve: Is that voice yourself or somebody else?

Pamela: It's—

Steve: I don't need to know who it is, but I want you to identify if it's your own voice—

Pamela: No.

Steve: Somebody else's?

Pamela: Umhm.

Steve: Listen to the tone and the timbre and the tempo and—

Pamela: Umhm.

Steve: —See if you can determine whose voice that is.

Pamela: Hmm.

Steve: Do you recognize that voice?

Pamela: (nodding) Umhm.

Steve: OK, so you know who it is talking? (In retrospect, I realize that Pamela already knew whose voice it was, so the steps of listening to the voice, asking whether the voice was hers or not, and so on was uneccessary. Even so, it was useful in getting her to pay close attention to the voice and her experience in response to it.)

Pamela: Umhm.

Steve: Great. Can you add the image of that person in with the voice, so that as you hear the voice talking, you see the person (gesturing with both hands in front of his face) who's talking to you?

Pamela: Umhm, umhm.

Steve: You can see them?

Pamela: Yeah.

Steve: Great. And you know who this person is?

Pamela: Yes.

Steve: Now I want you to expand the context, so that you not only see the person's face (gesturing with both hands close to his face) but the context (gesturing more widely with both arms), the larger context in which this person is speaking.

Pamela: Umhm.

Steve: OK? Does that make any difference, to see the person and to see the context?

Pamela: Yes.

Steve: Can you say a little bit about what difference it makes for you, without really saying much about the content of it, but is it more understandable, is it—?

Pamela: It's more understandable.

Steve: More understandable. So it makes more sense? (The context is a major determinant of meaning, providing the big picture that gives a broader perspective.)

Pamela: Umhm.

Steve: So again, that's a big progress away from confusion, right?

Pamela: Umhm (nodding). Yeah.

Steve: OK. Now, you know this—who this person is—

Pamela: Umhm.

Steve: —You know the context in which they're speaking.

Pamela: Umhmn.

Steve: Ask the person to clarify their message—

Pamela: Umhm.

Steve: —About this confusion and so on and, "Even though all these things are happening, life is meaningless," something like that or—is that the—I forget the exact words.

Pamela: Yeah.

Steve: What does this person mean by this? What does he or she mean by this?

Pamela: That, um, . . . everything is useless.

Steve: "Everything is useless." And can you explain—ask them to clarify more about this. This is kind of a summary, right?

Pamela: Umhm.

Steve: This is a conclusion about a lot of things.

Pamela: Yeah.

Steve: What are the things that this person is—has in their mind or in their memory, that leads them to this conclusion that life is useless? (This makes a distinction between the experiences and the conclusion about the experiences, which is a generalization about them.)

Pamela: You're—at the end you're all alone.

Steve: "At the end you're all alone." And again that's a conclusion. What is this conclusion based on? You know this person, right?

Pamela: Umhm.

Steve: You know their history? Something about their history, and what they've been through, and what they think about, and what's important to them, and so on?

Pamela: Umhm.

Steve: What led them to this conclusion? Don't tell me, I just want you to consider it.

Pamela: Umhm.

Steve: What are the factors—

Pamela: Umhm.

Steve: —In this that led them to this conclusion that life is useless and at the end you're all alone?

Pamela: Umhm. Umhm.

Steve: Does that make it more understandable?

Pamela: (nodding) Umhm.

Steve: You're having some feelings now, yes?

Pamela: (beginning to tear up) Yes.

Steve: That's OK. That's fine. They (gesturing to the audience) don't mind, I'm sure. Now, tell me a little bit about the feelings. Are they feelings of, kind of, acknowledgment or understanding of that other person?

Pamela: (nodding) Umn . . . sorrow.

Steve: Sorrow for that person?

Pamela: (nodding) Umhm.

Steve: OK, good. Stay with that a little bit. Sadness is a largely unacknowledged emotion. Sadness is different than anger and a lot of other things. Some things in life are sad. (To audience) I think it's sad that we all will need to depart the planet one day. I'm closer to that than most of you, probably. That's too bad. (This is an acknowledgment of her feelings, that also broadens the scope of things that are sad, joining with her, and normalizing her feelings.)

Pamela: Umhm.

Steve: So this message about life being useless is really a message about this person, isn't it? Is it about you or is it only about them? Or it could be both.

Pamela: Both.

Steve: Both. So you have a tendency to agree with this voice, right?

Pamela: Yeah.

Steve: This person? Close your eyes and tell them you agree with that. Does anybody have any tissues handy? We may not need them, but I'd like to have some, and I didn't bring any. (Someone in the audience offers tissues to Steve, who hands them to Pamela.) Just in case. OK?

Pamela: "I agree." I don't have to say it?

Steve: No, don't say it out loud.

Pamela: OK.

Steve: Just talk to this person and say, "I agree with you." And anything else that seems appropriate. (Pamela nods thoughtfully for some time as she does this.) Now again, I'd like to know if this results in any change—obviously you're having some feelings, the sadness and so on. Is it something that's sort of new for you or very old?

Pamela: Old.

Steve: And [would you] tell me more about the tears? If your tears could give words. We have some tissues there. (Pamela wipes her eyes with both hands.) What would your words say? What would the tears say if they were to express themselves fully?

Pamela: (holding the tissue to her face, crying) It's like . . . no way out.

Steve: "No way out." Out of what? We might be getting into some content here. Let me know if anything becomes too personal, or you'd rather not talk about it.

Pamela: No, no, it's OK.

Steve: OK.

Pamela: No way out of the black hole (yet another suggestion of depression).

Steve: "A black hole." Tell me about the black hole.

Pamela: It's like when you're in the ocean and you're swimming. I love to swim in the ocean. I love to get into the—under the waves, but there are times that you get caught in the—in certain holes (Pamela moves her body forward and down a bit) and they—

Steve: Umhm. Get pulled down?

Pamela: Yeah.

Steve: Get pulled down. OK. And what creates this feeling? In the ocean it would be the waves, but in your real life, is there some loss, some grieving? (Pamela nods.) OK. Is this the person that you lost? (Pamela nods again.) OK, good. I'd like you to imagine this person is here with us on the stage. And you can talk to them. (Pamela tilts her head down and puts her left hand on her face.) Can you do that? And tell them about your situation, that you feel that all is lost and life is useless and so on. And find out how they respond to you. Is this someone who died (Pamela nods) or just separated? Died, OK. So they're dead. I want you to talk to this dead person. (Pamela cries more strongly.)

Steve: What do they say back?

Pamela: (lifting her head) One [voice] says that—

Steve: (Someone in the audience gives Steve more tissues, and he hands them to Pamela.) There's some more here.

Pamela: (removing her hand from her face and raising her head) One says that (drying her eyes with tissue) he's waiting for me.

Steve: OK.

Pamela: And the other says that I should live.

Steve: I couldn't hear that.

Pamela: (removing her hands from her face) That I—I have to live. I should live.

Steve: OK. Great. Does that make sense to you?

Pamela: Hmm.

Steve: He's not in a hurry to reunite with you. Is that right? He or she?

Pamela: Yeah. He.

Steve: OK, it'll be simpler if I know that. So ask him for more advice. Tell him about how badly you've been feeling, feeling oppressed and in the black hole. Ask him for advice.

Pamela: He says he can't give me advice, because he has felt this his whole life. (So the person who died was chronically depressed.)

Steve: OK, so he felt it his whole life. (Pamela nods.) So he did not have a solution for his sadness and his sorrow?

Pamela: No.

Steve: Is that right?

Pamela: Umhm.

Steve: OK. Now, he's in heaven now (gesturing up), so he's got a good adviser. (Pamela puts her head down and smiles, almost laughing; the audience laughs. This intervention may seem a bit strange. However, it brings some humor into the darkness, while at the same time offering an opportunity for a different perspective that may be useful.) Ask him to check in with God— (more audience laughter).

Pamela: Umhm.

Steve: —Or whoever's important to you that way. And get some advice about how to live life, without the sorrow, without the sadness (pause).

Pamela: I can't find answers. The voice appears.

Steve: The other voice appears?

Pamela: There's two people.

Steve: Two people? OK. And tell me about the other voice.

Pamela: The other voice says there's, ah, many things going for me.

Steve: Oh, the positive voice? (Pamela nods.) And where is the positive voice? (Pamela gestures with her right hand to the left side of her head, at forehead level.) OK, over on your left side there (copying her gesture) and perhaps, what—a quarter of a meter away? (Using "meters" instead of "feet" seems like an inconsequential thing, but it is evidence that I am using her language, a small way of sharing her world.)

Pamela: Umhm.

Steve: OK. Yeah, about like that, great. And when you hear that voice, how do you feel? You can let the other voice go away for a little while (gesturing to his right). We can bring it back later.

Pamela: I feel better.

Steve: You feel better. OK. And ask it to clarify its message. In other words, if things are going [well] for you, ask it to amplify that in specifics about what's going well for you and so on. (Pamela bends forward and puts her head in her left hand and cries.) OK, now the other voice comes back? What's going on? (If she were thinking about how things are going well for her, she wouldn't be crying, so I know something else is happening, and I assume it is the other voice that makes her sad.)

Pamela: (crying, long in-breath) I made a promise. . . .

Steve: You made a promise.

Pamela: (raising her head and putting her hand down) to this person that I was going to— (putting her head in her left hand again).

Steve: That you what?

Pamela: —That I was going to be OK (her voice breaking, crying).

Steve: I still didn't get that.

Pamela: That I was going to be OK.

Steve: That you were going to be OK. OK.

Pamela: It has been very hard for me—

Steve: —To keep the promise. I see. So that makes you sad?

Pamela: Yeah.

Steve: OK. Talk to him again. Tell him, "I made this promise and it's very hard for me to keep the promise." (Steve's voice breaks on the last four words, as he empathizes with Pamela, a spontaneous and unmistakable nonverbal communication that he is feeling what she is feeling. In contrast, "I understand," said in a distant voice, would convey only an intellectual understanding.) What does he say . . . in return?

Pamela: To focus on the here and now, and not on the past.

Steve: OK. (Long pause, at the end of which Pamela draws a long in-breath and then exhales.) I'd like to go back to the more positive voice.

Pamela: OK.

Steve: Is that OK with you? (Pamela nods.) You have it up here by your head (gesturing to the left side of his head with his left hand.) Take that voice (gesturing with his right hand from the left side of his head to his chest and then to his belly) and put it down either in your heart or your belly. (Pamela puts her right hand on her belly.) Good. Does that make a difference in how you respond to it?

Pamela: No.

Steve: No?

Pamela: No.

Steve: OK. Is it OK to have it down there? Because I think it could be useful, but you're the judge.

Pamela: Yeah.

Steve: OK.

Pamela: It's a part of me.

Steve: Yeah, it's a part of you. It's a very important part of you. And you want it to be a strong part of you, and you want it to be inside you. The critical voices are better if they're outside, but the supportive ones are better if they're inside. Ask it to clarify what's going well for you. You may know it already, but I want you to hear it from this voice (Pamela wipes her tears with her left hand) because this voice is a reminder—

Pamela: Umhm.

Steve: —Of these things. It's like a friend.

Pamela: Umhm.

Steve: It's like an ally.

Pamela: Umhm.

Steve: So whatever happens, it can remind you of things that are going well for you. (Pamela continues to cry a little, and wipe away her tears.) (To the audience) Now there's something else I'd like to do that isn't quite on the program, but I hope it's all right with you if I follow my instincts and do what I think is going to be most useful for Pamela. (From this point on I will use a process for resolving grief [Andreas, 2011 & Andreas, 2002]. Rather than working with the voice itself, I will work with the experience of loss that the voice arises out of. The alert reader will notice that I haven't asked for the positive intent of the voice. I could have asked, and it might have been useful in changing Pamela's experience. The reason I didn't is because I understand that grief is always a reminder of good times that have been lost, and how important it is to acknowledge them and reexperience them. Unfortunately, the result is often sadness or depression. One way to make this obvious is to say to the grieving person, "I assume you know about amnesia, where someone completely forgets something. If you forgot that you ever knew this person, you would no longer grieve, right? Now here is my question, 'If I offered you that kind of amnesia, so that you had no memory of that person, would you want that solution.'" I have yet to find someone who wants that, pointing out the value in keeping the memory. The problem is how they have their memories, and this is what the grief process addresses, changing a sense of loss into a sense of presence.) (To Pamela) When you think of the lost person—can you give him a name? Is that all right? What's his name?

Pamela: Lucho.

Steve: Lucho? "Fight." (I happen to know that Lucho means "fight" in Spanish.)

Pamela: (nodding) Yeah, "battle."

Steve: OK. Where do you—if you imagine Lucho now—

Pamela: Umhm.

Steve: —How do you think of him? And here's what I want—well, here's what I need to know in particular. Do you remember him at one of the special times in your life? (Pamela nods.) Great. (To the audience) Because some people make the mistake of remembering the death or the ending of a relationship rather than the positive things of a relationship. (To Pamela) So you remember him in a good time? Tell me about the image—is it still, is it moving, is it big or small, and so on?

Pamela: Running. (Laughing softly) Jogging.

Steve: What?

Pamela: Jogging. Jogging.

Steve: OK, you see him jogging?

Pamela: Umhm.

Steve: OK. Well, that's the content. I want to know, you know, do you see him—

Pamela: Ah, moving.

Steve: Right, I understand that, but do you see him as if he's standing here or do you see him as a smaller picture or—?

Pamela: Just in front of me, like this. (Pamela first gestures in front of her at arm's length, and then turns and looks behind her, showing me Lucho's posture. I misunderstand and think that she is looking at Lucho behind her, and it takes me a while to realize my mistake.)

Steve: So he's around behind you?

Pamela: He's, he's like waiting for me. . . .

Steve: He's waiting for you?

Pamela: He's looking for me.

Steve: OK, so he's back here? (Gesturing behind Pamela.)

Pamela: (gestures with her right hand at arm's length in front of her, and then moves her hand toward her body.) He's looking back at me.

Steve: Is he in front of you?

Pamela: Yeah.

Steve: Oh, he's in front of you looking back!

Pamela: (laughing) Yeah.

Steve: I see! Good, got it. And is he life size?

Pamela: Yeah.

Steve: OK, great. Now (to the audience) this may not take as long as I thought (audience laughs). (To Pamela) Now, when you see him life-size there, can you enjoy the presence of being with him? (Pamela nods.) Great, so he's really with you all the time?

Pamela: Hmm.

Steve: Wonderful. Most people don't have that. Good job. Now, he's here life-size; you can enjoy the good feelings (Steve gestures back and forth between himself and Lucho, implicitly putting himself in Pamela's position in regard to Lucho) that you had with him, right?

Pamela: Umhm.

Steve: What have you lost?

Pamela: Smelling, touching.

Steve: OK, close your eyes. And reach out and touch him, or ask him to come closer if you need to. So that you can have the full experience of being with him, that he is present with you. . . . Is that a good experience? (Pamela cries softly, and nods.) Yes, good. I need to explain something to them [the audience]. You keep doing what you're doing, OK? Interact with him physically with touch (Steve gestures with both hands, as if touching Lucho) as well as seeing and hearing and so on. (To the audience) When people experience grief, they experience some kind of distance (gesturing in front of him with his right hand) between themselves and the dead person—or the lost person if it's a relationship and the person is still alive but they're not around. And when you reengage (Steve gestures in a movement that begins in front of him and moves toward himself) in all sensory systems—visual, auditory, kinesthetic—there is a reconnection, and there are tears of reconnection that are *not* the tears of grief. (Pamela dries her tears.) And I double check, because I don't know the difference. I can't tell from the outside, so I ask; I'm a dummy. But the tears of reconnection are lovely. They're reintegration. They're reconnection with an alienated part of the person. (To Pamela) Now, tell me a little of what's going on now.

Pamela: He vanishes.

Steve: What's that?

Pamela: He vanishes.

Steve: He vanishes? Where did he go to? Did he go to your heart? (Gesturing to his heart area.)

Pamela: (gesturing in front of her with her right hand at arm's length) He's always one step or two in front of me.

Steve: OK. Is that OK? Can you catch up with him?

Pamela: No (laughing).

Steve: Close your eyes. Talk to him and tell him, "Wait. Wait a minute. Come back." What prevents you?

Pamela: It's like—it's like we can't—

Steve: What's that?

Pamela: —It's like we cannot—it's so hard to—to reconnect.

Steve: "Hard to reconnect." OK. Now when I asked you to touch him a little while ago, you were able to do that.

Pamela: I could.

Steve: You did, right?

Pamela: Umhm.

Steve: And then did you did he separate again?

Pamela: Umhm.

Steve: OK, so you know how to do it—

Pamela: Umhm.

Steve: —But sometimes it's difficult?

Pamela: Yeah.

Steve: What makes it difficult?

Pamela: I don't know.

Steve: OK. Close your eyes.

Pamela: (reaching in front of herself) I try to catch something that I can't catch.

Steve: Yeah. But you caught it once—

Pamela: Yeah.

Steve: —Right here. Take a time travel back—3 minutes, 5 minutes—to when you were able to touch him and contact him. Do you remember that?

Pamela: Umhm.

Steve: Go back into that experience . . . and reconnect with him. (Pamela takes a deep breath.) . . . The memories that you have of this person, the positive memories, are yours. It would be a great loss if you were to keep him always at a distance. Whatever you had good with this person was yours, and the feelings that he aroused in you, the feelings that you elicited in him, all of those are part of your memory and part of who you are. It would be a real shame to leave these behind somehow, or to have them always running out of reach (gesturing in front of himself). So I want you to have them, and people often put them into their body in some way. Sometimes they put them into their heart (gesturing to his heart) so that they're always connected. Some people wear them like a cloak or a shawl (gesturing around his shoulders) around their bodies, so this is embracing them (putting his arms together in an encircling gesture). There are various ways of doing this.

Pamela: Umhm.

Steve: Notice how that would feel, if you try out different ways. (Pamela looks up above the horizontal for the first time in the session.) Or you can ask him (Lucho) "How would you like me to remember you?" (Pamela nods.) Do you have some way?

Pamela: Umhm.

Steve: Would it be all right for them (gesturing to the audience) to know about it?

Pamela: Sure. Here (gesturing with her right hand to her heart).

Steve: Right here? (gesturing to his heart).

Pamela: Yeah.

Steve: OK, good. Now, you have the feeling now in your chest.

Pamela: Umhm.

Steve: Is there anything that could take this feeling away?

Pamela: No.

Steve: I don't think so.

Pamela: No.

Steve: Not unless you forget. That would be very forgetful.

Pamela: Umhm. Yeah. . . .

Steve: OK. Pause for a little while and just experience that—what it's like to have him there in your chest, how your whole body feels. (Pamela uncrosses her legs, moves her whole body in a small stretch, and then settles down.) And I want you to remember that in every cell in your body, so that every cell in your body has a memory of how this is—how this feels to you. Now some people worry that if they have this feeling in their heart, in the chest, that they might not have feelings for other people, that it would get in the way. And it's not true. It's exactly the reverse.

Pamela: Umhm.

Steve: I'm just talking a little bit, partly for you, partly for them (the audience). That to have that feeling lets you know what you're capable of, lets you know what kind of relationship you want to have. Because at a certain point in your life, you're going to reengage with others in different ways as it's appropriate for you. And this feeling is not only a resource for you, but it's a guiding light. Does that make sense to you? (Pamela nods.) And whatever image you have of a guiding light, I'd like you to imagine that you put it in a little image that you put in your hand. So actually take your hand (Steve reaches out to Pamela's hand) and put an image in your hand—

Pamela: Umhm.

Steve: —Of whatever guiding light. What it's like to be in this relationship with Lucho. All the good things, all the good qualities—the humor, the connection, the tenderness, whatever. Different people have different relationships that they value. Whatever you value, put it on this card (Steve gestures with his hands) and then make it glow so that you can never forget. Now I want you to make it into a deck of cards, so you multiply it, and each one will be a little different. OK? And now I want you to do something very interesting. I want you to take this deck of cards (gesturing with his hands)—and they're all glowing, and each has a slightly different image and picture—and throw them out into your future (Steve's right hand moves in a throwing gesture in front of him) so that you can see those little spots of light (gesturing with his right hand at arm's length) leading you into the future. Is that nice?

Pamela: Hmm.

Steve: Most people love this. . . . OK, now if we go back to the original voice. What is it, "Life has no meaning," or—? If you hear that voice now, what is it like? (This is testing, to find out if the work we have done has made a difference in Pamela's response to the original troublesome voice. Although it is essential, and easy to do, it is woefully rare in most therapy.)

Pamela: Umm . . . less important.

Steve: "Less important." Is it true?

Pamela: (takes a deep breath) It's like it's there—

Steve: More a memory?

Pamela: —But it's a different feeling. . . .

Steve: OK. Yeah.

Pamela: It's—it's—(Pamela gestures in front of her with her right hand to the left and right, indicating the two voices) I can choose.

Steve: You can choose?

Pamela: Yeah.

Steve: I'd like to go a little further with this. I think we're almost done. (Pamela wipes her eyes.) Talk to that voice [that says] "Life is meaningless," or "Nothing makes sense."

Pamela: Umhm.

Steve: "Nothing makes sense. It's useless." Talk to that voice and say, "You know, do you really believe what you're telling me?" (Pamela nods.) And listen to their tonality, the tonality of that voice as it responds to you. Does it really believe what it's saying?

Pamela: Umhm.

Steve: It does. Do *you* believe what it's saying? (Pamela shakes her head.) No. OK, good. Tell them, tell them, that voice that, "You have your opinion; I have mine. I don't believe it. I have my Lucho in my heart—"

Pamela: Umhm.

Steve: —Or something like that.

Pamela: Umhm.

Steve: Do you have any questions about what we've done? Do you have anything unfinished that you'd like—?

Pamela: I think I have to just . . . (gestures with her right hand down the midline of her body in a slow gentle gesture) sink it in.

Steve: Yes, let it sink in. That's a good way, and I love your gesture. It's a wonderful, beautiful gesture (Pamela smiles) of very slowly—it's not this (gesturing down abruptly); it's not a lot of other things; it's a very gentle, very lovely flowing gesture, very nice. I need to explain one more thing, and partly for them (gesturing to the audience) as well—some of the logic behind this. If I think of my wife now, she is right here (gesturing to his left). Now I didn't think of her until I wanted to use her as an example. It's not like she's in my mind all the time (gesturing with both hands around his head) or something like that, or I'm hallucinating. But if I think of her, she's right here. She could have died an hour ago or two hours ago. (Pamela nods.) It doesn't matter.

Pamela: Umhm.

Steve: I can have her here with me, and the same is true of somebody who's lost somebody in the real world and they really have died.

Pamela: Umhm.

Steve: You can still have their sense of presence with you somehow. And that's a sort of intellectual explanation (gestures to his forehead)—

Pamela: Umhm.

Steve: —To hopefully make it easier for you to hold onto that feeling. (Pamela nods.) Do you have anything else?

Pamela: No, thank you.

Steve: I usually ask people (gesturing to the audience) if they have any questions for the client, but in this case I'd rather not. And you [the audience] can ask me questions and I can answer, but I'd like you (Pamela) to just sit down again there. (Pamela starts to get up, but Steve reaches out to her upper arm.) And before you go, thank you very much.

Pamela: Thank you. (Audience applause.)

Steve: And I'd like, when you sit down there, I want you to just stay with yourself. Put yourself in a bubble (gesturing with both hands around his head and torso) like you're in an egg, for a while, and just be with that sense. OK?

Pamela: OK.

Steve: Thanks very much. (Pamela gets up, embraces Steve briefly, and goes back to her seat in the audience. This session lasted a little under 34 minutes.)

Follow-Up

Several months after this session I contacted Pamela by e-mail and asked her how she was doing. She wrote back, "So glad to hear from you!! I am doing much better with my inner voices; I've been much happier. It has been easier to move forward. Thank you Steve, it was wonderful working with you!"

A year later I contacted Pamela again, and she wrote,

> My inner voices are still there, but they don't appear as often as before; after our session my anguish level diminished significantly. The voices appear today when I feel overwhelmed or demanded or very stressed. But mostly when I feel misunderstood by my partner or my children or significant people. That's when the voices torture me with "Nothing is worthwhile," "It's better to die, and to get it over it with," "Death is better than feeling the sadness." Most of the time I'm fine and happy. I don't feel anguished anymore when my partner has to travel; before our session I had separation anxiety and the anguish was awful.

This transcript illustrates several important principles. One is the key part that a troublesome internal voice can play in a very pervasive problem such as depression. Another is that working with the voice using this process is a way of discovering and understanding someone's internal experience. When someone uses a very abstract and general term like "depression," we really don't know much about what he or she experiences, because that word can be used for so many very different experiences. That is why I never used the word "depression" in talking to Pamela. When we find that the voice is above, and pushing down, saying, "Nothing makes sense; everything is useless," that tells us two very important things: (1) exactly how Pamela depresses herself, and (2) exactly what we can change so that she can do something different in order to feel better and have a more useful response to life's inevitable challenges.

6. Making Use of a Voice's Special Abilities

I'd like to begin this chapter with an e-mail that I received from a hypnotherapist in Kansas who read my previous book about changing negative self-talk (S. Andreas, 2012) and made good use of it. It is a lovely example of a way to augment the processes we have discussed so far, to make an even more useful change in a troublesome voice.

> I have used some of the techniques you gave us. I followed your instructions to find out whose voice this critical voice was. It was my mother's voice. She was always very critical of everything I did, and just about everything I said. I tried putting her voice out in front of me about three feet, then to the side three feet, and so on. I liked her over to my left about 15 feet. Her voice is easier to ignore over there. Then I just imagined her sitting on this wooden fence that we used to have in our back yard, sitting in an uncomfortable position, in a straight skirt, just as she used to really do. She would wear straight skirts all the time, even when gardening and raking, or even working in the garage.
>
> I pictured her balancing herself on that wooden fence, holding a clipboard, trying to be involved in all that I do, but not really being able to from over there. To tell you the truth, it was hard to do that, because I always wanted to please her, and I know she would rather be inside me, deciding everything for herself. I used to let her be in there. Of course, I didn't know I had the choice to easily move her out like this.
>
> I can remember her inside me in high school. I would see everything through her eyes, and wonder if she would approve. I thought it was pretty crazy, so I didn't talk about it. I assumed that she didn't approve of my actions, and felt uncomfortable most all the time in those days. When I was older, once she told me she was very proud of me, and I didn't know what to do with that piece of information; it made me feel as uncomfortable as when she would disapprove. I think in the days she was raising me, they didn't think much of complimenting kids. I know she told me you were never supposed to tell a little girl that she was pretty, because that would spoil them.
>
> At first after I put her over there on the fence, she still made comments I didn't need to hear. Then one day I was in the car and needed to remember some things and couldn't find a pen or anything to write on fast enough. I turned to her in my mind and said, "Mom, will you write this down for me?" She seemed to be delighted to be needed, and kept the notes for me! Soon after that, she just drifted away as a judge. She appears from time to time as a companion and a good friend, though. She's been dead for years, of course. (Carol Henderson, personal communication, 2010)

Once you have gained some distance from a troubling voice, so that you don't feel overwhelmed and overpowered by it, the communication that had been one-way can become two-way. You can talk with the voice, and begin to influence both how it speaks to you and what it does, in order to improve your life.

In this chapter I want to focus on what Carol wrote in the last paragraph of her report: "She seemed to be delighted to be needed, and kept the notes for me!" Just like people in the real world, the voices of the people that we remember inside us like to be useful and appreciated for their skills and abilities, and we can benefit from making use of these skills.

In this example, the context of driving made it hard for Carol to take notes—a simple and easy task that she could easily do at other times—but easy for her "mother" to do, because she wasn't driving. You might think that this is a curious and perhaps humorous way to make use of an internal voice, and not realize that the principle underlying this simple example is potentially much broader and more useful. You can ask an internal voice to help you with any situation that you find difficult, but is easy for the voice to do, because it has the relevant ability. This can go far beyond writing some notes for you while you are driving.

When the voice has a positive intent for you, it already wants to help you. Offering it another way to help you serves this positive intent, making it even more useful and valuable, so the voice nearly always answers yes. If occasionally the answer is no, that doesn't have to be the end of the exchange. It can be the beginning of a conversation about how you would really value and appreciate its help, explore the voice's objection to helping you, and so on.

Even when the voice's positive intent had nothing to do with you, it may be willing to help you. Our internal voices don't like having nothing to do, and often they will be happy to take on an additional task in order to be useful and appreciated.

I assume that in the course of reading this book thus far you have already been working with a troublesome voice of your own, and have identified whose voice it is, clarified its message, and found its positive intent. You are now in alliance with it, and can interact with it in a friendly way. If you haven't yet done this, please find a troublesome voice of your own now, and use it to go through the exercises in the previous chapters, so that you can get the most benefit from the outline below—a process for asking a voice for assistance.

Asking a Voice for Help

1. Identify the voice's abilities. Listen to the voice and see the person who is speaking. What are this person's strengths and abilities? Everyone—even people who are very limited—has some activities that they are not so good at, and others where they excel. What was this person really good at? It might be a special skill or ability like planning ahead, or it might be a really

useful cheerful or tenacious attitude that carried him through difficult times. Pause now to consider what that person was particularly good at, and make a brief list of those skills. . . .

2. Give appreciation. Now speak to that person, and give him or her some appreciation for his special abilities. "You were really able to show your concern for other people's problems, and point out possible solutions that they could try out." . . .
3. Give thanks. If you have learned one or more of these useful abilities from that person, give some thanks for what you learned. Be specific about what you learned, and mention one or two specific situations in which it has been useful to you. "Mom, I learned from you how to get inside other people's heads and understand what their experience is like. That has been particularly useful in my teaching, to figure out what was missing in a student's understanding." . . .
4. Identify an ability that you didn't learn. Now think of that person's other abilities that you didn't learn. Pick one that could be particularly helpful to you in certain situations. "You were always good at spotting what's missing in what someone says, avoiding being misled by others. I never learned how you did that." . . .
5. Ask for help. Now ask that voice if it would be willing to assist you whenever you are in a situation where that ability would be particularly helpful to you. The voice could be useful to you in a variety of ways, from noticing when something needs attention, suggesting what needs to be done, keeping track of finances, comforting you, offering you specific words or information, and so on. "Would you be particularly vigilant in noticing what I am missing, and alert me anytime you think I might be in danger of being misled? That could keep me out of a lot of trouble, and I would really appreciate your help." . . .
6. Testing. Think of a specific situation in the past where you would have liked to have this kind of assistance, and that might occur in the future. . . . Then simply run a movie of that event and find out what happens. If your voice offers useful information, give it some appreciation. If the voice doesn't help you, have a conversation with it to find out what needs to happen so that it will be willing to offer help, and then test again. Repeat this as often as you find necessary until it is satisfactory. . . .
7. Congruence check. Turn inward and ask, "Does any part of me have any objection or concern about the changes we have made?" Notice any feeling, visual image, or auditory sound or voice in response to your question that could indicate a problem. Usually there will be no objection, because the voice is glad to help and get some appreciation for what it knows how to do well, and the result of this will be to make your life better. If you notice anything that could indicate a problem, first check

to be sure that it really does indicate an objection, and then find out what you can do to satisfy the objection, so that you can reach congruence.

Making use of a voice's special abilities in this way is only a systematic process for doing something that you have been doing since very early childhood. We all learn from others around us, from playing dress-up as small children to deliberately learning a particular skill from a parent, teacher, or coach. Although we may consciously decide to copy someone else's abilities, much of our actual learning is unconscious, rather than conscious. We learn not only the explicit teachable aspects of a skill or ability, but also how that teacher moves and breathes as they do it, and all the other nonverbal behaviors that would be hard to notice or describe consciously.

Even when we don't consciously decide to learn from others, we are automatically learning from all the information that our eyes and ears and body are sensing. Some of the skills we have learned from others are identified in our minds as being things that others do, rather than things that we can do. Sometimes this is a useful distinction, because we may not want to do some of the things that others do—it wouldn't fit with our values and goals in life. Even if we don't smoke, our knowledge of how to strike a match and light a cigarette is recorded in our images of what Uncle Fred does. Sometimes we may not have learned something very useful and desirable from others because we had some limiting belief like, "Oh, she's so talented; I couldn't learn to do that." When that has happened, we can always use our remembered internal images and voices of someone else to learn a new skill for ourselves—even many years after that person has died and is no longer available in the real world.

When we have made peace with a voice, and have even given it some additional useful things to do for us, it may sometimes still be unpleasant and difficult to listen to. It may be too loud and intrusive, or have a tonality that is whining or grating, so it can be useful to make some further adjustments in how or when the voice speaks to us, to make it easier to listen to.

In the next chapter, I explore how to collaborate with a voice in finding a more pleasant and useful way to speak to you in order to carry out its positive intent. In the real world, a trusted friend who has your best interests at heart is someone you can always listen to attentively, no matter what he or she says. You can discuss anything, express yourself fully, and make use of each other's knowledge and wisdom. You can utilize this kind of voice in the same way in your internal world, a shortcut for making a voice easier to listen to and communicate with.

7. Using the Voice of a Trusted Friend

When you have joined with a troublesome internal voice, retrieved information, clarified it, and discovered the positive intent, you know what the voice wants to achieve by talking to you. Because you've identified the positive intent behind the voice, that means that you agree with it, so you and the voice are now allies. You may still not like the way that the voice talks to you, but you are in agreement with what it wants to accomplish. Since you are in agreement with the intent, you both want to communicate more effectively. That agreement makes it much easier to adjust how the voice carries out its positive intent—by changing the words, location, volume, tempo, or any other qualities of the voice that you find unpleasant to listen to. That might seem to be a difficult thing to accomplish, but it is actually quite easy, because every positive intent actually has three aspects.

The Different Aspects of Positive Intent

Every positive intent—whether it is for the person speaking, for the person the voice is speaking to, or for someone else (or any combination of these possibilities)—there are always three different aspects of that intent, and two of them may not be immediately obvious:

1. The positive intent itself, the desired goal or outcome of the communication, what the voice wants to accomplish—protection, improvement, expressing a feeling of love or concern, and so on. The other two aspects of positive intent are about the intent itself.
2. The desire to communicate the positive intent to someone else. This desire to communicate is a very useful aspect that can be leveraged to alter what the voice says and how it says it. If a voice communicates in a way that you are more willing to listen to, that will satisfy the voice's desire to communicate with you. For instance, if the voice is screaming loudly, or has a mean and sarcastic tonality that makes you feel bad, you can talk directly to the voice as if it were another person. "Look, I'd be much more willing to listen to you if you would speak more softly, or with a more friendly tonality." Since this alternative way of talking supports the voice's desire to communicate with you, the voice is motivated to at least consider your request. And when the voice actually tries out a different tonality and finds that you do indeed listen to it better, that is convincing evidence that the change will better serve the voice's positive intent—a win-win change that benefits you both.
3. The voice's implicit desire to be acknowledged and appreciated for its positive intent. Just as parents or friends want to be recognized for their positive efforts, a voice wants to be appreciated. When you sincerely thank a voice for communicating,

> its need for appreciation is satisfied. That makes it even more willing to change how it communicates, because if it communicates more effectively, it will get more appreciation.

When you ask a voice if it would consider using a different way of speaking, sometimes it may be concerned that it will be restricted to the new way of communicating, so it's very important to reassure it. "I am not proposing to take any old choices away from you; I'm only asking you to consider adding a new one. If I don't listen well when you use a more pleasant tonality, you can always go back to yelling at me."

One way to proceed would be to identify each aspect of the troublesome voice that makes it unpleasant to listen to, and ask the voice to alter each of those aspects in turn. This might require changing only one or two elements, such as the volume or the tempo, which would be fairly easy to do. However, it's possible that this could require identifying many different aspects of the voice that makes it difficult for you to listen to it, and choosing an alternative that would be more comfortable for you. If there were a lot of these, it could take some time to identify and change each one.

Luckily, there is a way to change most or all of the troublesome aspects of a voice at once, in a way that is perfectly tailored to you. Almost everyone has at least one trusted friend, someone whom you would be willing to listen to, because you know that they have your best interests at heart and want your life to go well. If a voice that was originally troublesome were to use the voice of your trusted friend, you would be happy to listen to it and listen to what it has to say to you, no matter what it had to say, or how it said it.

This tone of voice will carry a package of tonal qualities that are comfortable for you to listen to, and that will instantly and effortlessly convey a host of very useful presuppositions and implications, including friendly alliance, positive intent, safety, comfort, and also all the positive experiences you have had with this person that elicit your willingness to listen to him or her. Many of these presuppositions and implications will be unconscious, and it might take days to consciously identify all of them. If the voice that has been troublesome would use that tone of voice, it would automatically elicit more useful and positive responses in you.

Usually it will be better to choose a trusted friend of the same sex as the original voice, because some people might find it strange to hear their father speaking in a woman's voice, or their mother using a man's voice. If you can't find a trusted friend of the same sex, you can try using the voice of a friend of the opposite sex as the original voice, and find out if that is OK with you. Some people find this a bit weird and don't like it, while others find it acceptable, even if it is a bit strange at first.

One of my friends is very matter-of-fact, so he can say, "You sure messed that up" in a neutral tone that isn't condescending or judging. Another friend is more positive, gently suggesting what I could have done instead. "Next time, it might work better if—" and I am happy to listen to either one of them. Now if you think through several of your friends, who has a voice that you feel most comfortable listening to when they offer you suggestions or feedback?

The voice that you choose might be one that someone else would find annoying or unpleasant, but as long as you are happy to listen to it, it will work for you. I have often used the voice of an old college buddy, who was more than a little sarcastic. When I goofed up, he would say, "Nice work!" However, whenever he said this, he was always smiling, and I knew that he was still a good friend who knew that he often screwed up too, not a superior critic putting me down. Someone else might find that voice abusive and annoying, but for me it works perfectly. That is the importance of asking for a voice that works well for you.

If you can't easily think of a trusted friend—living or dead—you can use the "as if" frame to elicit what such a trusted friend would sound like if you did have one. "If you did have a trusted friend, of the same sex as this voice, someone who you knew wanted the best for you, someone whom you would listen to, no matter what the person had to say, how would that person's voice sound? . . . Would it be soft or loud? Would it be slow or fast? Would there be a special tonality that was like a smile or a chuckle in that voice? What would it sound like?"

The voice of your trusted friend might still include some elements that could be improved to make it even more comfortable to listen to. Perhaps the friend speaks very slowly, so that it is a bit irritating to wait for him or her to finish a thought, or there is a regional accent that you would prefer not to listen to. Then you can ask the voice to please speed up a bit, or soften the accent so that it is more pleasant to listen to, or to use a different accent, and so on.

The exercise outline below presupposes that you have already gathered more information about a voice, clarified what the voice wants to say to you, and discovered one or more positive intents that have to do with you—the voice wants to offer you guidance, support, or some kind of protective warning, and so on. Perhaps you have already asked it to help you with its special skills, as discussed in Chapter 6. If you haven't already done all this, please back up to previous chapters and do so before taking your voice through the process below.

Using the Voice of a Trusted Friend

1. Select friend. "Think of a trusted friend, of the same sex as the voice, who you know cares for you and has positive intent,

someone you would be willing to listen to carefully, no matter what she or he said." . . . This presupposes that the voice that is selected will have those qualities, and will elicit appropriate positive responses in you.

2. Listen to the friend's voice. "Listen carefully to this friend's voice—its volume, tempo, tonality, and so on. Particularly notice the unique qualities that distinguish this voice from all the other voices you have ever heard." . . .
3. Ask the troublesome voice to adopt this tonality. "Would you be willing to try using this voice of my trusted friend, whom I would listen to attentively no matter what the content is? I am not asking you to give up the choice of using the tonality that you have been using. I'm only asking you to try an alternative to find out how well it works. You will always have the option of using the old tone of voice." . . .
4. Testing. If the voice says no, there must have been a miscommunication earlier, so you need to back up to an earlier step and clear up the misunderstanding before moving forward again. Assuming that it responds "Yes," ask it, "Please try out that voice now, to find out how well it works." . . .
5. Thank the voice. Assuming that the voice uses the friend's tonality, thank it sincerely. "Thank you for using that tone of voice; that is much more pleasant and easy for me to listen to." . . .
6. Adjustments. Make any further adjustments that would be useful. For instance, if the voice is still a little too loud, you might ask it to be a little softer. Or you might want to adjust when it communicates with you, so that it talks to you before some activity, or afterward, but not during the activity because that would distract you and interfere with what you are doing. . . .
7. Rehearsal and testing. "Imagine a future situation in which you might want this voice to speak to you, and find out what happens spontaneously." . . . If it uses the trusted friend's voice, well and good; if it doesn't, you will need to ask the voice for more information, to find out what the problem is. Either there was a miscommunication earlier, or the communication is clear, but there is some objection to the change.
8. Congruence check (sometimes called an ecology check). "Does any part of me have any concerns or objections to any of the changes we have made? Is there some problem with using my friend's voice? What would have to happen for you to be willing to use my friend's voice in this future context?" . . . Often an objection indicates that there was some confusion or miscommunication at an earlier step, so you might need back up to a previous step in order to clarify it. For instance, the voice may think it is committed to using the new tonality forever, rather than that it is an alternative to try—only as long as it works

better than what it had been doing previously. At other times, objections identify real problems that might occur as a result of the changes that have been made. For instance, in certain noisy contexts you might not be able to hear a very soft voice, so it would have to speak louder so that you can hear it clearly. . . .

9. Satisfy objections. There are three different ways to satisfy an objection that may arise when you ask a voice to change:

    a. Adjust the changes so that they no longer interfere with one or more other important outcomes that you have. "Choose the voice of a different trusted friend, or adjust the voice that you have already selected, so that it works better for you."
    b. Carefully contextualize the changes so that they don't occur in any contexts in which they might interfere with some other important outcome. "Hearing this trusted friend's voice is only appropriate in my personal life, not in my professional life, where it could cause trouble."
    c. Reframe or recategorize the meaning of either the changes or the objection to the changes, so that there is no longer any conflict between your outcome and the outcome of the voice. "You object to having this person speak using your friend's voice because you think you might lose track of reality. But actually it is a sign of creativity and flexibility; crazy people are very rigid and uncreative. And as long as you don't tell anyone about this voice, it won't concern others."

    Or, of course, you can use any combination of the three kinds of modification above—either simultaneously or sequentially. . . .

This process is something that you can use with any voice, saying any words whatsoever, and without revealing any content publicly. And you can guide someone else through the process, even if you have very little background or understanding, as long as you follow the steps in order, and pause to allow them to actually experience each step.

At the end of this process, you will have an internal voice that has the same positive intent as the original voice, using your trusted friend's voice. What it says will often become more positive, so you will be much more willing to listen to it and hear what it has to say to you. You and the voice are now even fuller allies, and you can collaborate in making any further changes at any time in the future. You can negotiate how it speaks to you, what sort of useful advice or information it offers you, when it offers that information—or any other adjustment that would improve its communication with you.

8. Putting It Together—Again

In the first three chapters we explored how to join with a voice, retrieve and clarify information, and discover a voice's positive intent. Then, in Chapters 4 and 5, I offered transcripts of two examples of putting all these processes together into a systematic sequence. In Chapters 6 and 7 I discussed two additional processes that can make this process even stronger and more robust—how to ask a voice to help you with its special abilities, and how to utilize a trusted friend's voice to transform how the voice communicates with you.

Now we can add these last two processes to the previous sequence to create a process for transforming a troublesome voice that is even more complete, as presented in outline in the appendix. You can use this process yourself, or you can offer to guide someone else who is suffering from a troublesome internal voice. Since this process doesn't concern itself with content, you can use it with any voice—no matter what words it says, or how it says those words.

I offer yet another transcript because each time I use this process with someone, I use somewhat different words or examples. Each person also responds to the process in his or her own way, and needs extra guidance from time to time, to clarify misunderstandings, or to respond to questions, and so on. This transcript is from a training session in which participants had not had the kind of prior instruction that I have provided in this book. As a result there was initially more ambiguity and confusion than usual, and it took some restraint on my part not to ask for content—what the man's voice was actually saying. Although that would have made it easier for me to understand his experience, it would have made it harder for participants to follow and learn the steps of the process itself. From time to time Ray misunderstands what I am asking him to do, giving me many opportunities to notice when he is going off track, and I need to ask questions or give him instructions to bring him back to what he needs to do to make good use of the process.

Steve: I would like to have someone up here who would like to go through a process to demonstrate working with some kind of troublesome voice. This will be content free. We just talked about the importance of content sometimes, but this will be content free. It will be a process, just like many other processes that you've learned. And I'd like to have someone come up here and do that. (Several people raise their hands.) OK, I think you're first. (Ray comes up to the front of the room.) OK, I'd like you to think of a troublesome voice.

Ray: Got it.

Steve: Got it? That didn't take long. Well, you probably already had one sitting down there. Listen to it carefully, learn more about it, make friends with it, to the extent that that's possible. I know that it's troublesome, so probably your first impulse is to go away from it, but I'd like you to really listen to it, listen to its tonality, the tempo, hesitation, the unique qualities of that particular voice. (To the group) And this is scope, right? Getting more detail, going toward something, getting more data. Scope provides more information.

(In this seminar I had organized all my teaching around the fundamental concepts of scope and category, which are described in great detail in my book Six Blind Elephants Andreas, 2006a).

Ray: It's kind of hard to do.

Steve: What makes it difficult?

Ray: I think it's ambiguous, but it's all-encompassing.

Steve: All right. So, is what it says all-encompassing—a "universal quantifier" kind of voice? (A universal quantifier is any word like "always," "never," "every," that makes a sentence apply universally, throughout space and time, to every context.)

Ray: That's my interpretation.

Steve: OK. . . . Can you explore the ambiguity further? Just notice how it's ambiguous. Is it what it says? Is it an ambiguity in the voice tone?

Ray: It's separate from content.

Steve: It's separate from content—so, it's just the voice tone? Or tonality? Or all those things? I'm going to call it "tonality" for all the auditory qualities, OK?

Ray: OK. As I look at it—

Steve: You look at it?

Ray: Look at it—

Steve: How do you do that?

Ray: It's kinda weird, because I'm looking at it, but it's undefined and the voice is very, very clear, but it's not—it's dissociated, so the message that I hear is clear—

Steve: OK, so you can hear the words.

Ray: I can hear the words.

Steve: And the tonality?

Ray: And the tonality, yes.

Steve: OK. But when you go for the meaning of the words? Is that what's not clear?

Ray: No. That's really clear.

Steve: That's really clear. So what is it that's not clear?

Ray: A connection to. . . .

Steve: A connection to your behavior?

Ray: Kinda like the words are there, but the part of me that is very aware of the words—that they affect me, but I don't see a voice,

I don't see—what they are connected to. It's like I can describe it—it's like on a time line—and this being younger, there's like a voice, and it goes like in a circle and it's like brown, and there's a voice that comes out of it—a very clear voice, and then I'm over here looking at it saying, "You have way too much power." (The voice appears to be coming from an abstract brown circular representation, separate from the person who said it, and separate from any context.)

Steve: OK. So that's an evaluation or a description, about the voice—right? That's a categorization of the voice.

Ray: Right

Steve: OK, that's great. That's important. Sure. OK. And, you know, if it didn't have power, it wouldn't trouble you, right?

Ray: Right.

Steve: Great. OK, that's fine. Good. OK. Now I want to ask you, "Is this your voice or someone else's?"

Ray: Someone else's.

Steve: Someone else's. Great. (To the group) Now if he said it was his voice, I would say, "Who does it remind you of?" or "Where did you learn to talk in this way?" or something of that nature. I mentioned that yesterday. Great. OK, so you know who it is.

Ray: Mmhm.

Steve: Great. OK. That's good data. And now I want you to see that person in that context, where they're talking to you—see their face, and perhaps their whole body, but certainly their face and their upper torso, so that you can learn more about their facial expressions, their—the way they hold their head, the way their lips move, etc. What can you learn more about this, in the visual system, in this context? And really explore that for a little while. Is that clear?

Ray: Mmhm.

Steve: OK. Take a little time. . . . (To the group) Often when people are troubled by a voice, it's out of context, and you've forgotten sometimes who it was, even. And this brings more scope, brings more data.

Ray: It's interesting because the person who I saw—his voice—his face is kind of soft. (Ray's voice rises on the word "soft," indicating questioning surprise.) It's incongruent with the words.

Steve: It's surprising somehow.

Ray: Yeah.

Steve: OK, good. That's good information. So there's some kind of incongruity there.

Ray: Umhm.

Steve: OK. Great. Learn a little more about that. And as you do that, you can expand your scope even more to the larger context. Where are you? Are you in a room in a house, are you outdoors fixing a car, or—just what is the larger context of what this voice is saying to you, what this person is saying to you?

Ray: Like seeing it there being said? Or just—

Steve: No, what's said is the same, and you identified the person who said it, and I just want to know—where, when—I don't need to know—but I want you to expand your frame so that you see where you are—

Ray: Mmhm, OK.

Steve: —And what's going on around—what's the context in which this voice said that.

Ray: I've got a couple here, so—

Steve: OK. Well, just pick one. It doesn't matter. You probably, maybe, have hundreds. If it's a parental voice, for instance, this may have been said to you many, many times. Just pick one.

Ray: OK, got it.

Steve: OK. Great. So you've got the context. Look around in the context a little bit. What is that like?

Ray: The context is really cool, because—

Steve: No, I don't need to know about it. I just want you to get it.

Ray: OK.

Steve: OK. Great. Now I'd like for you to notice the speaker's limitations. You know this person, right?

Ray: Mmhm.

Steve: Think about their limitations. It could be genetic, it could be accidental, it could be tradition, it could be familial, you know, history, family history, personal history, mistakes, lack of intelligence, or lack of communication skills—you name it. Just think about how they are limited in various ways in the context of this communication.

Ray: It can be anything from—

Steve: Well, again, I don't need to know—I just want you to know—to pay attention to them, actually. . . .

Ray: OK.

Steve: OK, great. Now I want you to ask that person if they would be willing to clarify their message. There's some ambiguity there; there's this incongruity between the expression on their face that you mentioned, and the message that they sent. Imagine that person is in the room, and you could talk to them, and you could just say, "Would you please clarify your message? Given all I've noticed—I've noticed all these incongruities," or whatever it is. "Can you clarify your message? What is it that you want to say to me?" Or "What is it you really want to say to me?" That's another little piece. What do you really want to say? That's sort of a meta-outcome piece. "What do you really want to say to me?"

Ray: Mmm.

Steve: And listen to what they answer.

Ray: Having trouble. . . .

Steve: OK, what's the trouble?

Ray: That part of, "What do I really want him to say?"

Steve: No, it's not what you want him to say, it's what does he want to say to you.

Ray: What does he want to say—OK, I got it.

Steve: He said this to you in a way that was very troublesome and ambiguous, you said.

Ray: OK.

Steve: What does that voice want to say to you, that it said somehow confusingly, or in a way that made it hard for you to understand?

Ray: OK. . . .

Steve: Got that? Is that interesting?

Ray: It is interesting because it is so out of character.

Steve: What's that?

Ray: It is interesting because it's so out of character; it's almost like I'm hearing it, but—can't believe it. (This is a nice indication that he is actually getting a message from an unconscious aspect of himself, in contrast to consciously trying to figure it out.)

Steve: "Can't believe it." OK, that's all right. You clarified it. Good. OK. So there's still some incongruity.

Ray: Mmhm.

Steve: OK. Fine. OK, ask that person for their positive intent. This should be familiar to you. "What did they want to do, what did they want to accomplish by saying this to you, that was positive?"

Ray: OK.

Steve: Got that? You got the positive intent from that person?

Ray: Mmhm.

Steve: Does that make sense to you? . . . (Ray moves his head back and forth, left to right.) Sort of.

Ray: "Sort of."

Steve: (to the group) Did you see his head tip back and forth? That means "sort of." You know that one—most of you—but still, it can help your communication if you notice that—and you can pace it and respond to it. Is there more positive intent? Ask him if there is something else that would clarify or resolve the uncertainty, or the ambiguity.

Ray: Mmhm

Steve: Got that? Is it clear now?

Ray: Yeah; it's good.

Steve: OK, great. So now there's no ambiguity, is that right?

Ray: Mmhm.

Steve: OK, great. I want you to thank that person for being so willing to communicate with you, for offering this additional information. . . . Is this someone you know pretty well?

Ray: Yes, very well.

Steve: OK. A little earlier I asked you to think of this person's limitations. Now I want you to think about their special skills and abilities. What was this person really good at? Take some time to make a mental list of these, because we're going to do something interesting with it.

Ray: OK. . . .

Steve: OK, you have a list now?

Ray: Mmhm.

Steve: Now give that person some appreciation for their skills: "You are really good at—" and mention at least several from your list. . . .

Ray: OK.

Steve: Now look through this list, and ask yourself, "Of these skills and abilities, which ones did I learn from this person?" . . .

Ray: OK.

Steve: Now thank them for what you learned from them. "Thanks for teaching me—"

Ray: (hesitating) Well, I learned a lot of not-so-useful things too.

Steve: I'm not surprised, but we can deal with those some other time; just stay with what you learned that was valuable, and give thanks for that—even if the learning process was uncomfortable, as long as the resulting skill is useful to you. . . .

Ray: OK.

Steve: Now ask yourself, "Which of this person's skills did I not learn, or at least not very well? Which do I lack, or am I weak on? Which of this person's abilities could be a resource to me, because I'm not very good at that?"

Ray: OK. . . . I've got two.

Steve: Great. Talk to this person, and first compliment them on these two skills: "You're really good at ________ and ________, and I'm not." . . .

Ray: OK.

Steve: Now ask that voice, "Would you like to be a resource to me by offering me helpful advice at appropriate times and places? You could be a sort of coach who would offer me specific knowledge and suggestions about what to notice, say, or do, so that I could learn to become more skilled? I would really value and appreciate that." . . .

Ray: That person looks eager and pleased. He seems to really like that idea.

Steve: Great. Now let's test this. Think of a situation in the past in which you really could have used one or both of these abilities. Put yourself back in that situation, and find out what kind of advice or suggestions this person offers you. . . .

Ray: Yeah, he did, and that really made a difference in what happened next, and how things turned out better as a result.

Steve: Great. Now do the same in the future; think of a possible future situation where you would welcome some assistance, and find out what kind of advice or suggestions this person offers you. . . .

Ray: OK. Got it.

Steve: OK, great. Next I want to ask you to do something that can sort of wrap up everything we have done into a sort of package that can make it even smoother and easier for you. If your voice is already communicating well, it might not be necessary, but I would like to offer it to both you and the group, because it can sometimes make a big difference. Can you think of someone of the same sex as the voice, who is a trusted friend, someone who you know has your best interests at heart—someone like an old high school buddy, a spouse, or someone whom you trust, and you would listen to no matter what they had to say to you, and no matter how they said it—it would be important for you to listen to them because you know there is this foundation of trust and good will? . . .

Ray: Mmhm.

Steve: Got somebody like that?

Ray: Yeah.

Steve: Is this a man or a woman?

Ray: A man.

Steve: Great, listen to his voice for a little while. Listen to the qualities of his voice. What makes him individual? The kind of thing where you pick up the phone and someone says, "Hi," and you already know who it is because of their tonality.

Ray: OK.

Steve: Got that? OK, Great. Now I want you to go back to that person we have been working with, and ask him if he would be willing to use the voice of your trusted friend in the future. . . .

Ray: Mmhm.

Steve: OK? Is he willing to do that?

Ray: Mmhm.

Steve: Ask him to try it out right now. Whatever he wants to say to you right now, he can use that voice of your trusted friend. . . . (Ray nods.) Pretty interesting?

Ray: That was cool.

Steve: It was cool. OK, good. Now do the same thing, and imagine in the future, that this voice might want to communicate something to you, perhaps whatever the positive intent was of the message that it communicated to you in the past—perhaps many times. Imagine some time in the future when this voice might want to communicate with you, and just kind of check it out. (To the group) This is future-pacing; it's also testing—is it still speaking in that voice?

Ray: And this would be the original—

Steve: Well, it's the original person, but speaking to you in the voice of the trusted friend in the future. So just check it out and make sure it works. . . . OK? (Ray nods.) Great. Now do you have any concerns or objections? Do a congruence check. It looks like it's all very smooth and everything's cool—

Ray: OK.

Steve: Check real carefully, though; kind of check throughout your body for any feelings, make sure there's no little voice somewhere, crying in the wilderness, that has some concern about this. . . .

Ray: (confidently) No, it's all good.

Steve: All good? OK, great. Thanks very much.

I spoke to Ray four days later, and he said, "Thanks again. It really gave me a new and powerful perspective on an old and outdated voice."

A detailed, 21-step outline of this process can be found in the appendix. The process demonstrated in this transcript can be done with any content whatsoever, and without revealing any content publicly. With very little background or understanding, you can guide yourself or someone else through the process, as long as you understand the steps and follow them carefully. Of course, each person is different; sometimes you can skip a step or two, or do some steps in a different order, and still have a good result. Chapter 9 provides an example of using many of these same principles, but in a different style and sequence, to get the same kind of positive results.

9. Putting It Together—in a Different Way

For ease in learning the approach I am presenting, I have offered a detailed sequential process. Like practicing scales in music, this is a way to build skill and understanding. However, the basic principles of joining, communicating, and offering a voice other options to consider can be used in other ways. The transcript below of a session with therapist Douglas Flemons illustrates many of the principles and processes presented in this book, yet in his own unique style, and using somewhat different language.

I include this somewhat lengthy transcript for a number of reasons. It shows that I am not the only one using this approach, which is quite different from more widely recognized methods. It also shows how the same principles can be used in a different and more "free-form" way than the sequential protocols that I have presented. Finally, it offers me rich opportunities to comment on aspects of therapeutic work that I wouldn't otherwise think of.

This transcript was published before we met and found so much in common in our approaches. Douglas's comments in the original chapter are indicated by parentheses ( ) and my comments appear in *italics*. Note that while many of Douglas's comments are explanatory, some describe corrections—what he wished he had done instead. I point this out because it shows that he is focused on continually reviewing and improving what he does, something that is all too rare in the field of therapy.

Work at Altering, Rather Than Negating, Your Client's Symptoms[1]

Most of us are unsuccessful at achieving lasting relief by banishing a scary thought, controlling a painful sensation, silencing a critical voice, squelching a troubled memory, or numbing an overwhelming emotion. In fact, by virtue of our attempts to control or negate something that's troubling us, we can end up inadvertently and undesirably connected to the very thing from which we passionately wish to separate.

If people persist in, and/or intensify their disjunctive efforts with an undesired chunk of experience, it will take on leechlike qualities, becoming a symptom or problem capable of frustrating any attempts (theirs or a therapist's) at controlling or eradicating it. Recognizing this relational quality of language and mind, you'll do best to organize your therapy around accepting and altering, rather than opposing or negating, their symptom.

Carrie and her husband Sam both agreed that Carrie was "hyper-vigilant" about keeping her sons safe and well—so much so that she was constantly distraught that one of them would catch a cold or sprain an ankle. At its worst, Carrie's

---

1 *Of One Mind: The Logic of Hypnosis, the Practice of Therapy* by Douglas Flemons. © 2001, by Douglas Flemons. Used by permission of W. W. Norton & Company, Inc., pp. 227–233.

worry was debilitating for her and restrictive for her boys; she would constrain their activities way beyond what they and Sam thought was remotely reasonable. But despite their protestations, nothing could dissuade her from taking extra measures to keep her family safe. Nothing, indeed, could keep the severe voice in her head from whispering, "Did you do enough?"

[Notice that there is a huge deletion in Carrie's voice, namely the criteria for "enough." Without criteria, she can never know when she has done enough, so she can never relax her vigilance. One way to work with a voice like this is to ask, "Enough for what?" in order to elicit the missing information that provides a context and the criteria for being able to decide when she has done enough. There is a detailed example of doing this in my client session video, "You're Not Good Enough" (S. Andreas, 2010b).]

Carrie could quiet the voice for brief periods by heeding all its admonishments and demands, but it remained ever wary, always prepared to reproach her for making the tiniest little slip. And if she mustered the temerity to reassure herself that she was doing a good job, she'd be subjected to withering criticism. Sam worked hard to reassure her of her positive qualities, and this sometimes helped temporarily, but if the voice considered her the least bit neglectful, its invective would become unrelenting.

I invited her into hypnosis in the last half of the second session. Carrie decided she wanted Sam to stick around, though she was initially uncomfortable with his looking at her. I suggested they both focus on the same spot in front of them, as if they were watching a movie together. Since they were both watching the same movie, her concern that Sam was watching her was no longer relevant, and this helped Carrie relax into the experience. *[This is a nice example of making a simple change in order to satisfy an objection.]*

Then, as I commented on ambient sounds, speculated about possible thoughts and sensations, and offered possible experiences, she stopped bothering to distinguish herself from me, her body, and her surroundings. Tears appeared occasionally on her cheeks.

When she reoriented to the room at the end, she said that while I was talking, she was seeing an image of herself at thirteen, sitting on the floor in her room next to her bed, looking at her closed door and feeling incredibly sad.

[Note that she is seeing herself, not being herself, a way of maintaining some distance from her sad feelings, protecting herself from their full impact. This spontaneous image provided a context that added to the meaning of what the voice had been saying.]

Not having planned or attempted to evoke any memories, I was surprised and encouraged by the spontaneous freedom of her response. Noting that sadness is different from anxiety, I scheduled the next appointment.

When she and Sam returned the following week, Carrie said that she'd woken up the day after our last session feeling more peaceful and hopeful than she had in years. We talked about her sensitivity, and about the interesting way emotions evolve when freed up to be themselves. After inviting her into trance and telling her a story about being at the movies with my wife, I suggested that she, too, could focus her attention on a screen in front of her, watching what happened and filling me in on the details.

Carrie: I see my mother in my room. Her back is to me. She's angry. (Like the week before, we were back in her room, but this time she wasn't alone.)

[Although Douglas's initial suggestion to Carrie was to focus on a screen in front of her, as if watching a movie, she is now seeing her mother rather than herself, implying that she is seeing out of her own eyes—in the movie, not watching it.]

Douglas: How can you tell she's angry? (Had she used past tense, I would have invited her into using present tense, but she was already ahead of me.)

Carrie: She just is.

Douglas: Is it the tension in her back, the tilt of her head, her body position? (I prefer descriptions to conclusions, as they offer readier opportunities for transformation.)

[This is a very important distinction; directing her attention to the details of what she is experiencing increases the richness of that experience; additional information facilitates a change in meaning or conclusion.]

Carrie: She's above me. She's big.

Douglas: How old are you?

Carrie: I don't know—thirteen, fourteen, maybe fifteen.

Douglas: Are you sitting or standing?

Carrie: I'm sitting on the floor by the bed.

Douglas: And how can you see her anger? How can you tell?

Carrie: In her mouth. (pause) Her mouth is angry and her eyes are disappointed.

Douglas: And where is she?

Carrie: In the room. I'm looking up at her. (Sitting on the floor, looking up: a vulnerable, submissive position.)

Douglas: All the way in?

Carrie: She's partly in. She always passes by me. She's distant. She's not close. She's always disappointed in me. I can't be the way she wants me to be.

Douglas: How is that?

Carrie: She wants me to do things like her, do them her way. (pause) I can't do that. She's so sad. She misses me, too. (What a wonderful opening! She spoke the words "I can't do that" with a tone of guilty defeat, but they held the potential for personal assertion and integrity.)

[By exploring this scene in detail, Carrie spontaneously notices her mother's inner feelings rather than just her anger, providing a different perspective than she had at the beginning.]

Douglas: Go inside and find that voice of yours that's wise enough to know that, despite your mother's pain, her disappointment, her sadness, her anger, despite all that, it's necessary for you to do things your way. Go and listen to that voice, that necessary, wise voice, and tell me what it's saying. (long pause)

["Find that voice of yours that's wise enough" presupposes that she already has this wise voice, and that it is "wise enough" to know that "it's necessary to do things your way"; it is only a matter of finding this voice.]

Carrie: I can't find it. Her (mother's) voice is so loud. (In the first session, Carrie had described trying unsuccessfully to "brush the voice away." But even if she were to manage to briefly brush it off, this would only encourage it to fight back. The key was to find a way to alter it, not negate it.)

Douglas: Well, it's important to be respectful of your mother's presence, so you don't want to try to shut up—to shut out what she is saying—but it is difficult to hear two things at the same time. (pause)

[The implication in the last part of the previous sentence is that Carrie could easily hear one voice at a time.]

So go ahead and turn down the volume of her voice so you can hear yourself think. (long pause)

["Turn down the volume" is the first of a number of direct suggestions to change process aspects of her experience of her mother's voice.]

My mother used to come to my door and yell, "Turn that music down! I can't hear myself think!" That was good motherly advice: Turn down the volume so you can hear yourself think. So go ahead and turn down the volume of your mother's voice so you can hear yourself think.

[In this metaphor, Douglas introduces the idea that a mother can also provide good motherly advice.]

And you might as well lower the illumination on her as well, so you can see better, too.

["Lower the illumination" is another direct suggestion to diminish a process element of her experience.]

Nothing like a little subdued lighting and background music to encourage self-reflection.

["Subdued lighting" has connotations of intimacy and friendship. Decreasing the volume of the voice, and decreasing the illumination, will make it easier to attend to Carrie's internal wise voice. "Background music" is an indirect suggestion to add a pleasant supportive tonal background to her experience.] (long pause)

Now go inside again and tell me what you can hear that wise voice saying.

["Tell me what you can hear" presupposes the rest of the sentence, "that wise voice saying."]

Carrie: It's saying, "I am smart!" (She sounded defensive. I was concerned that if the defensiveness remained, her definition of herself as smart would stay bound—that is, logically and experientially tied—to her mother's accusation that she wasn't. Since I didn't want her positive assertion to automatically invoke its negation, I looked for a way of easing the two apart, of creating a protective insulation—a gap of insignificance—between them. If the assertion "I am smart" could exist on its own, with its own existential integrity, then it could endure and be enhanced regardless of what the mother put forth.)

Douglas: Fine. What is the quality of that voice? (pause)

Carrie: It is angry.

Douglas: Sure, for good reason. *[This is a nice acknowledgment and acceptance of her anger.]* Go ahead and take the anger out of that wise voice and listen again. (pause) Now how does it sound? (long pause.) (I wish I hadn't been so abrupt. Rather than trying to snatch the anger away, I should have given it an opportunity to evolve into some other emotion. Or I could have suggested that she let it increase, and as she felt it rising higher and higher, she might begin to notice it pulling another emotion into the light. And as this other emotion appeared and developed, the anger, having been so helpful, could now be free to continue on its way, out the door, through the ceiling, into the ether, or whatever. Oh well.)

[The alternatives that Douglas offers are excellent. Although the instruction to separate the anger from the voice was abrupt, it was preceded by fully acknowledging the anger when Douglas said, "Sure, for good reason." Carrie's response indicates that she did not experience it as abrupt or intrusive, so I think it was useful. An alternative would be to ask, "What is that anger saying?" or "What does that anger want for you?," acknowledging the anger, while at the same time inviting it to express itself more fully and transform into something else—without specifying what it would transform into.]

Carrie: It (the wise voice) sounds calmer. Freer and calmer.

Douglas: Right. And now what's happening?

Carrie: Is it true? What if I'm wrong? I'm scared.

[Notice that at this point, Carrie uses "I'm" for both, indicating that she is alternately identifying with both the wise voice and the scared voice, which are in opposition.]

Douglas: OK, well that, too, is an important voice *[A nice acknowledgment.]* so listen carefully to it, as well. And like the other voice, allow this voice to tell you its important message.

[This sentence is an instruction to separate from the voice and listen to it, and "allow" presupposes that the rest of the sentence, "tell you its important message," will occur if Carrie does not interfere with it. Asking for the message of the voice shifts attention from the fear to the message of the fear.]

Notice that, as you listen to it, respecting it, the edge can come off it. (long pause) *["As you listen to it" presupposes both "respecting it," and that "the edge can come off it."]* And now how does it sound? (pause)

Carrie: Smaller.

Douglas: OK, but don't let it get too small, because it is important that it has a conversation with the voice that is saying, "I am smart." So go ahead and let them converse (pause) and tell me what happens. (long pause) (I made the assumption that if instead of trying to quell the voice of fear, she were to listen to and respect it, it wouldn't have to be so loud.)

["Let them" presupposes the rest of the sentence if Carrie doesn't interfere. Earlier Carrie identified with the voices but at this point, both voices are separate from her. "Conversation" and "converse" imply a friendly exchange, rather than an oppositional one.]

Carrie: The scared voice says, "I don't want to mess up," and the smart voice is reassuring it.

[A very useful intervention at this point would be to ask the scared voice to change its message from a negative one, "I don't want to mess up," into a positive one, such as, "I want to succeed," "I want to be accepted," "I want her to love me," etc.]

Douglas: I have a suggestion for the smart voice.

["Smart voice" ties together the voice and its behavior. It would have been better to say, "the voice that says, 'I'm smart,'" to separate the voice from its behavior. A "smart voice," like a "smart kid," always has to be smart, but a voice that says "I'm smart" has the freedom to say, and be, many other things as well.]

(At this point I personified the two voices—a way for me to demonstrate my respect. I talked to the smart one directly and used the pronoun "her" to refer to the scared one.)

[Personifying the voices is a way to respect and acknowledge them; it is also a way to separate them from Carrie. Using the pronoun "her" also achieves separation, so that Carrie can be more objective. Again, "smart one" and "scared one" join the voice and its behavior; it would be better to say, "the voice that says I'm smart" and "the voice that is scared," so that they both have the freedom to be different at other times and places.]

Douglas: I wonder what would happen if you were to (pause) reassure the scared voice in a different way—if you didn't try to settle her down. If you respected her for helping you be smart.

[The last sentence presupposes that the scared voice is not in opposition to the smart voice, but actually helps Carrie "be smart," a very useful shift from being in opposition.]

So I wonder what might happen if you were to reassure the scared voice that you won't let her disappear, reassure her that she keeps you smart, (pause) that you'll always listen to her because she makes you smarter.

[Within an "as if" frame, "what might happen," Douglas presupposes that it will be useful for the smart voice to support the scared voice. The two voices can both support each other, healing the remaining division between them.]

(I then switched back to talking to "Carrie," rather than the "voice.")

Douglas: Go ahead and let the smart voice tell the scared voice something like that, and let me know what happens. (long pause)

["Let the smart voice" presupposes that the rest of the sentence will happen if Carrie doesn't interfere with it.]

Carrie: The scared voice isn't scared any more. Just sad.

Douglas: OK, listen to that, and wait to see how it continues to change. (If you accept and respect your clients' nonvolitional response, not trying to negate it, and building the expectancy that it will transform, something—who knows what?—will happen.)

["Wait to see how it continues to change" is not really an "expectancy"; it presupposes not only that it will change, but that it will continue to change.]

Carrie: (long pause) Now it is peace.

Douglas: Peace. Yes. And now what?

Carrie: Bright.

Douglas: What sort of brightness?

Carrie: Like the sun. Very bright.

Douglas: Now is this just the scared voice that has become this, or—?

[At this point it would be better to say "the voice that was scared," or "the voice that used to be scared," since it is no longer scared. Saying "the scared voice" will have a tendency to reelicit the fear.]

Carrie: No.

Douglas: —is it possible to even identify the smart voice and the scared voice separately? (pause) (My "even" heightened the likelihood that they'd be experienced as one.)

[Again, saying "smart voice" and "scared voice" will have a tendency to reverse the process.]

Carrie: No.

[This is a nice confirmation that the suggestions for integration have been successful—despite the use of "smart voice" and "scared voice."]

Douglas: Well, how appropriate that smart and scared together would be bright. Very bright. (I don't know whether her imagination was punning on the double meaning of bright, but even if it wasn't, I couldn't resist.)

Carrie: It is filtered now, like through trees.

Douglas: So there are some shadows, too?

Carrie: Yes.

Douglas: Oh, wonderful, for shadows are important, too. You always need both the brightness and some shadows, some dappled light and shadows. (My comment allowed me to offer again, this time metaphorically, the idea of embracing, rather than expelling.)

Douglas: Now put this in a safe place within you, a place that you can always return to. And your dreams at night can continue the process here. Have you found a safe place to keep this?

["Now put this" presupposes the rest of the sentence—that there is a safe place within her that she can always return to, and that the process can continue in her dreams.]

Carrie: Yes. (She smiles.)

Douglas: OK, so now go back to your room and look up at your mother. (pause) And now what's happening? (I wanted to give her an opportunity to "road test" whatever changes had occurred, by returning her to the scene with her mother, and find out if it has changed in a useful way.) (pause)

[Although this kind of experiential "road-testing" is essential in finding out whether or not an intervention has been successful in changing a client's response, it is woefully rare in most therapy.]

Carrie: She's so sad.

Douglas: Yes. And can you notice what happens to you *["Notice" presupposes that something will happen to her.]* when you allow her sadness to be hers? *["Allow" presupposes that what follows "her sadness to be hers" will occur if she does nothing to interfere with it. This implies that Carrie doesn't have to experience her mother's sadness, only her own. Notice that Douglas does not try to change the sadness into happy feelings. Sadness at the lack of communication between her and her mother is a valid response to be acknowledged, in contrast to the fear she had been experiencing, which is now gone.]*

Carrie: I'm sad, but it's OK.

Douglas: Yes. You can give her the freedom to be sad. And this is a freedom for you too, isn't it? *[Feeling sadness is acknowledged and recategorized as freedom, both for her mother and also for her.]*

Carrie: Yes. (pause) It's OK.

Douglas: OK, well, you can return to this room now, bringing with you the sensations of having had a restful nap.

Five weeks later, when they returned for their last appointment, Carrie told me she no longer heard the voice (The severe voice that previously said, "Did you do enough?") and no longer felt "the oppressive weight" she'd always carried around. She felt more confident, more sure of what to do, and her worry was, she said, "within normal limits."

10. Protecting Yourself From External Voices[1]

Throughout this book I have assumed that our internal voices originate in what we have heard from others at some time in the past. When we heard supportive, loving, and encouraging voices, we incorporated them into our lives, using them to feel good and solid about who we are and what we can do, even when those people are not around to offer their encouragement and support. Unfortunately, we also often took in troublesome voices that criticized, belittled, or terrorized us, and we may also hear those voices when the people who put us down are not actually present. Throughout our lives we have been nourished by supportive voices, and "polluted" or "infected" by troublesome ones. No book about troublesome voices would be complete without some instruction about how to protect yourself from the toxic voices of others to begin with. If you are protected from them, you will be much less likely to internalize them and suffer from what they say.

Many people experience a troublesome voice not as the set of sounds and words that they are, but as if it were a physical thing, as if a knife had been plunged into the heart. They take in the meaning of what is said without any kind of protection or evaluation, and instantly feel terrible, even when the voice is saying something that has little or no basis in fact.

Many people know intellectually that what others say is only their opinion, which might or might not be true. ("Sticks and stones can break my bones, but words can never hurt me.") However, very few can actually hear an insult without responding with bad feelings, because they don't have the protection that a secure boundary would provide. They still feel hurt by a criticism; they still feel anxious when someone talks about a possible danger; and they still feel depressed in response to someone saying, "Life has no meaning." Fortunately, you can learn how to protect yourself by developing an effective personal boundary. A strong boundary can enable you to use the methods in this book in the moment. When someone says something to you, you can pause to join with it, see it in the larger context of time and space, clarify the message, determine the positive intent, evaluate it all, and then decide on an appropriate response. But first you need a durable boundary to protect you, so that you feel comfortable doing this.

Personal Boundaries

You have probably had the experience of being uncomfortable when someone is too close to you, and you feel as if he or she is intruding into your personal space. You can probably also think

1 This chapter is adapted from Andreas, S. (2002). *Transforming Your Self: Becoming Who You Want To Be* (ch. 13). Boulder, CO: Real People Press.

of times when you felt distant from someone, and wanted to feel closer. Each of us has a comfortable distance for interacting with someone else—not too close, yet not too far—and this varies considerably depending on the person, culture, activity, or context.

If you are with a stranger, or someone who has caused you difficulty, you probably want to keep your distance from that person. When you feel safe with someone, you can comfortably allow the distance between you to shrink, perhaps to nothing at all, allowing intimate physical contact. These experiences are a clear indication that we all have a personal boundary, and also that it changes in response to different contexts or events.

Your boundary is not something that you learned or developed consciously and deliberately; it is something that you learned unconsciously, by trial and error, from chance events, comments from parents and others, the idioms of the language you learned, and the nonverbal responses of others. Because of this somewhat random acquisition, no boundary is perfect, and I have yet to find someone whose boundary works as well as it could.

Some people have a boundary that works quite well, while others don't. Some people have a weak boundary that leaves them always feeling unsafe and vulnerable to the slightest comment or other intrusion. Others have such solid boundaries that they have great difficulty relaxing into close and intimate relationships. Many others have a boundary that is somewhere in between these extremes, or that alternates between them.

The first step in creating a boundary that protects you well is to find out what kind of boundary you already have. You can do the exercise below by yourself and learn a lot. However, if you ask a couple of willing friends or family members to do the exercise with you, you can learn even more, because of the contrast between your experience and that of others. Each of you can discover how different your boundaries are from the others, and these alternatives can point out possible ways that your boundary could be changed to make it more effective.

Another alternative is to explore your own boundary first, and then ask several other people the same set of questions, to find out how their boundaries are different. This is another way to discover alternative ways of having a boundary that you can try out yourself. Even when you try something that makes your boundary less effective, you can learn from that, and quickly change it back, or change it in the other direction. For instance, if you try making your boundary close to your skin, like a suit of armor, you can learn how restrictive that feels, and then move your boundary out farther from your body until it feels comfortable.

Some people worry that they might try something and not be able to change it back, but that concern is as valid as what some parents tell children to try to keep them from making ugly faces: "Some day your face will freeze, and you'll look like that for the rest of your life!" For years I have had a favorite saying, "You can play with your mind without going blind." Only changes that fit well with all aspects of who you are will be lasting, and of course that is what you want.

Boundary Discovery Exercise

Close your eyes now, and think of someone with whom you feel very safe, and notice what it is like for you to be with that person. . . .

Now notice if there is any boundary between you and that other person, and if so, what is it like? . . .

Now for contrast, think of someone whom you feel very unsafe with, and notice what it is like for you to be with that person. . . .

Probably you can sense some kind of boundary that separates you, in order to protect you. What is your boundary like in this situation? . . .

Now examine your boundary in more detail. What is it made of, and how does it protect you? . . .

Does it surround you on all sides, or only in front of you? . . . Does it also protect you from above and below? . . .

How far away from your body is it? . . .

How thick is your boundary? . . .

Is it hard and rigid, like glass or steel, or is it more flexible, as if it were made of rubber or soft plastic, or more like a magnetic energy field, or a kind of radar? . . .

Does it have a color or sound? . . .

What does it protect you from well, and what are its weaknesses or drawbacks? . . .

Just as a short experiment, imagine that you are with this person you feel unsafe with, and allow your boundary to dissolve or disappear, and notice how you feel when you do this. . . .

You probably felt much more vulnerable when you did this, showing how your boundary protects you. This protection makes it possible for you to feel resourceful and behave in ways that are different from how you would respond if you had no boundary. It may seem strange than an imaginary boundary has such a strong effect on your feelings, but this is true of many of your other internal images and thoughts.

Since no one I know was ever explicitly taught as a child how to build an effective personal boundary, each of us had to build our boundaries in a pretty haphazard and unconscious way. Through trial and error, some of us managed to create a boundary that works reasonably well, while others didn't. However, I have never yet found a boundary that was perfect—even a really effective boundary can be improved. Now that you have learned what your boundary is like, you can experiment with changing any of these aspects that you have found, and notice if that makes your boundary more or less effective in protecting you.

For instance, a boundary may be very effective at keeping distance from others' pain or disturbing feelings, but not very good at protecting from others' words. Changing the boundary so that it changes the sound in some way can add protection from those words. If you imagine that the boundary is made of something that muffles the sound, or changes its volume or tonality in some other way—for instance, as if you were hearing it through a wall, or underwater, or from an old tape recorder—you may find that it is much easier to listen to the words without having to respond immediately with strong feelings.

Boundary Experimentation Exercise

Next I want you to experiment with what you have already discovered. Simply change the boundary that you have in different ways—change its color, density, distance, thickness, material, sound, and so on, and find out if each change makes you feel safer, or more vulnerable.

When you find that a change makes you feel more vulnerable, either change it back, or try an opposite change. For instance, if making your boundary thinner makes you feel more vulnerable, try making it thicker. Whenever you find a change that works better for you, keep it.

You may find that sometimes a change makes you feel safer but also has some other effect that you don't like. If that happens, see how you can find a way to have the added protection, without the side effect that you don't like. For instance, making your boundary thicker might make you feel safer, but then you can't see through it as well, and you don't like that. Perhaps if you made the boundary more transparent, or lightened the color, or changed the hue, or made the boundary tougher or more flexible instead of thicker, this problem would no longer occur.

People vary enormously in what makes a boundary more useful for them. For one person, a bright blue color works best, while for someone else, a dark green or red will work better—and I have no idea why this is true. Despite a great deal of individual variation in what works well, a few general principles apply for most people.

General Principles

1. Distance. Many people's boundaries are too close to their skin, so anything that penetrates the boundary is immediately threatening. Your boundary will protect you better if it is farther away from your body, giving you plenty of time to prepare a response

to any threat. When I am walking in a rough part of town, my boundary is at least 30 feet away from my body, and becomes a sort of radar that alerts me to any danger long before it can get too close.

2. Flexibility. It's best if your boundary changes automatically in response to events, so that it can expand away from your body, or strengthen in situations of danger, and then quickly diminish in strength—or even disappear—when you are in a very safe situation. A flexible boundary can adapt appropriately to any situation, and change quickly when the situation changes.
3. Toughness. If a boundary is made of something hard and brittle, it may crack and shatter catastrophically in response to some threats. When someone says that he "fell apart" or was "shattered" by some event, that is not just a metaphor; it is an accurate report of how he felt when a boundary failed to protect him. A boundary that is more resilient, like rubber or a magnetic energy field that can absorb a shock without breaking, will usually work much better.

Now think of a challenging situation in which you have felt vulnerable in the past, and experiment further with changing your boundary in the ways I have suggested. Discover for yourself what changes in your boundary would protect you better. Whenever you find a change that works well, keep that and then go on to find out what other useful changes you can make.

Since others will usually have very different boundaries than you do, when you ask them about theirs, that can offer additional alternatives to try out, to find out if they are useful to you. And you can always continue to experiment whenever you want to, and revise your boundary whenever you think of or discover a possible improvement.

Once you have a boundary that works well for you, one of the ways you can add to it is with a process that my wife and I developed many years ago. When someone criticizes you, your boundary can "catch" the words and either print them out visually on the boundary itself, or in the space between you and that other person, transforming the auditory message into a visual image of the words.

You can read those words hovering in space, and go through a process of evaluating them and deciding how to respond. In the visual modality, it is easier to keep the message "at arm's length" so that you can respond to it with a lot more logic and much less emotion. Since you are safe, you can comfortably take time to think about the events that those words describe, and decide if that description matches your experience or not. If not, perhaps you don't understand what that person said well enough, and you can ask her to clarify what she said. "You just called me a creep, but I'm not sure exactly what I did that led you to that conclusion; can you clarify that so that I can understand?" Or perhaps on reflection you realize how that description points out aspects of something you did that you hadn't previously been aware of, and that you might consider changing.

After you fully understand what that person is talking about, you can decide how you want to respond. Perhaps an apology is in order, and perhaps also a commitment to change how you respond in the future. Perhaps you and the other person simply have different views, and you are not yet able to come to a mutual understanding. Or perhaps you decide that the other person is drunk, schizophrenic, or severely limited in some other way. Since that person's response arises almost entirely out of his or her limited experience, it really has little or nothing to do with you or your behavior. Whatever your response, it comes only after a careful process of evaluation, rather than being an automatic and unresourceful knee-jerk response.

This entire process has been described in more detail, including a verbatim transcript of teaching it to a young man, Carl (Andreas & Andreas, 1987). Twenty-six years later, Carl reports that this process is still working for him, and that he has taught it to his children. With an effective boundary, you can be protected from being a helpless victim of what others say, and avoid taking in more troublesome voices from outside.

11. Not Talking Back

In previous chapters I have often warned against opposing a troublesome voice with another more supportive one, because of the internal conflict and incongruence that inevitably creates. Instead, I have offered many ways to change a troublesome internal voice to avoid this kind of conflict altogether. I wanted to offer you ways to change voices that do work, rather than discuss methods that don't.

However, a number of well-known and widely respected experts and therapies strongly advocate talking back to a troublesome internal voice as a way to lessen its influence, so no book about troublesome voices would be complete without discussing this opposite approach. For instance, Richard Bandler—one of the original developers of Neuro-Linguistic Programming—advocates answering a troublesome voice with a loud repeated internal mantra, "Shut up!" to overcome a troublesome voice with sheer volume. "Often we say nasty things to ourselves and criticize ourselves continuously. To change this, we can learn to interrupt these negative thought patterns by repeating a mantra. My favorite mantra is 'Shut up!' because it works so well" (Bandler, 2008, p. 88).

If you internally say "Shut up!" loudly every time you begin to hear a troublesome voice, it certainly does make it difficult to hear it and pay attention to it—and if you can't pay attention to it, you won't feel bad, so it does have a certain utility. Try this out in your own experience to confirm that it does work. You probably know the first words that your troublesome internal voice says, or the tonality that indicates that it is beginning to criticize you. As soon as you hear those words or tonality, shout "Shut up!" internally to drown it out. . . .

A troublesome voice is typically autonomous, speaking without conscious invitation. If it were under your conscious control, you could just choose to be silent, so it has to be an expression of an unconscious part of you. In contrast, saying "Shut up!" is a conscious and voluntary response in opposition to the unconscious one. After a number of repetitions, this response can also become as automatic and unconscious as the original troublesome voice.

However, there are several very serious drawbacks to this method. Pause right now to try it out, and you can easily discover at least some of them. . . .

If you didn't discover much in the experiment above, check out Bob Newhart's (2010) video skit, "Stop it!" on You Tube, which humorously illustrates a very similar method.

Since your internal voices are echoes of the voices you have heard externally from others, they will tend to respond in much the same way as other people do. If you were to shout "Shut up!" to someone else in the real world, what would the response likely be?

Usually the other person would shout back, or escalate the conflict in some other way.

If you are in a position of power, he or she might meekly fall silent, at least temporarily, but this would not resolve your differences. Even when a voice meekly falls silent, it is likely to speak up again in the future—perhaps "behind your back"—or change what it does so that it is not so easily noticed and confronted. For instance, it might switch to using a quick sarcastic "Riiight!" to undermine your thinking and functioning at unexpected and inconvenient times. Opposing an internal voice can actually make that voice stronger, which is probably not the outcome that you had in mind.

Another downside to this approach is that while the internal shouting match is going on, you can't say anything useful to yourself, because there is too much noise. If there weren't so much internal racket, you might be able to talk to yourself in a more useful and supportive way. For instance, you might say something like, "Given all the factors in this situation, what do I want to do?" or "I know I can figure this out," directing your attention and behavior in a positive and useful way. An internal shouting match will make that difficult or impossible.

Yet another drawback is that despite its unpleasantness, there is at least a possibility that a troublesome voice might have a positive intent, and some useful information for you. As I pointed out in Chapter 3, usually an internal voice wants to protect you from some kind of problem or danger, even if this is expressed as belittling or criticism. And of course the danger may be one that was real at sometime in the past, but isn't at this time.

A voice might want you to notice a mistake, so that you can improve what you do. A voice that says, "Boy, you really screwed up that interview!" wants you to do better. What a voice says may be unpleasant, and may even be counterproductive, but it usually has the positive intent of making your life better in some way. A voice could be warning of an actual physical danger: "If you try that, you could get seriously hurt." Or it might caution you against being disappointed, embarrassed, or criticized by others—dangers to your status, or your idea of who you are. "Don't make a fool of yourself at the party tonight."

If you were to simply drown out a voice by saying, "Shut up!" you would lose the useful positive intent—throwing out the baby with the bathwater. Many people desperately need some kind of warning internal voice, because they keep making the same mistakes over and over without noticing. Losing a protective voice can have much more unpleasant consequences—especially long-term—than hearing an unpleasant internal voice and feeling bad in the moment.

Creating Internal Conflict

The most serious drawback in opposing a troublesome voice by saying something like "Shut up!" is that it creates an internal conflict between the troublesome voice and the voice that says "Shut up!" If someone has been a helpless slave to an internal voice, this kind of conflict may be a useful first step forward, a start toward breaking out of prison. But if you don't go further, it leaves you with an internal battle between two opposing sides. Most people already have plenty of internal conflicts; they don't really need yet another one.

Of course, two internal voices can also have a friendly and useful conversation, just as two friends can cooperatively discuss what to do about something. For instance, when you are considering different factors in an important decision, one voice might say, "Well, I think it would be good to go forward with that purchase because—" while another might respond, "OK, but if we do that, we also need to be sure to think about how we'll pay for it, and the consequences." Just as two people can cooperatively discuss a decision, two (or more) internal voices can collaborate in reaching one. The conversation will last only as long as it takes to reach a satisfactory conclusion.

However, typically a troublesome internal voice is critical, scornful, or berating, rather than cooperative. Answering it by saying, "Shut up!" will quickly set up a battle rather than cooperation. This battle will likely be repetitive and chronic, rather than temporary and limited to a particular topic. Some people have been battling troublesome voices for many decades without any resolution.

Many people seek help because they already have chronic unpleasant internal conflicts like this. A common troubling conflict is between some version of "Be sure to do what others approve of," and "No, be independent and think for yourself." A conflict like this often puts you between a rock and a hard place, because whatever you decide to do, afterward the other side will torment you. "You just went along with the crowd again, you wimp," or "You sure blew it with that racy joke you just told."

Another common conflict that we all face daily is between indulging in a present pleasure on one side and its future consequences on the other. One voice may say seductively, "Go ahead and treat yourself by eating that dessert; you deserve it," while another warns, "If you eat that, you'll get fat, and no one will want to be around you." Whether or not you eat the dessert, the other side will badger you with the consequences later. "You denied yourself a simple pleasure that would have made you feel really good," or "Now you've done it; you'll have to struggle with what you eat all next week in order to lose the calories in that cheesecake you just ate."

In the late 1960s, I learned Gestalt therapy, developed by Fritz Perls, and wrote *Awareness* (Stevens, 1970), a book of exercises and processes based on Gestalt therapy principles. I also edited two books by Fritz Perls, *Gestalt Therapy Verbatim* (Perls, 1969a) and his autobiography, *In and Out the Garbage Pail* (Perls, 1969b). At that time, my name was John O. Stevens, a name I changed when I married my wife, Connirae Andreas.

A fundamental method for resolving an internal conflict in Gestalt Therapy is to ask a client to sit in one chair and express one side of a conflict to an imagined person or entity in another chair. Then the client switches chairs and responds with the other side of the conflict. The client takes turns switching chairs, identifying with and becoming each side. Acting out the conflict in this way often took a long time, and it was frequently punctuated by weeping, shouting, pounding pillows, and smashing chairs, before finally sometimes reaching resolution. If Perls had realized the usefulness of eliciting the positive intent, Gestalt therapy would have been enormously more efficient and effective.

Despite the noise and the broken furniture, and the lack of eliciting positive intent, the two-chair process has three very useful aspects. One is that it clarifies that every internal conflict is between the person and someone else—even if that someone else is labeled "society" or "the church," or some other entity. It is a way to separate the two sides of the conflict, and to clarify each one. This process has sometimes been called externalization, and it can be a very useful first step toward resolution.

When a client says something in one chair that has difficult implications, subtle accusations, or with some other kind of a "hook" in it, when they switch chairs, they have to respond to these, often clarifying the disturbed relationship between the two parts.

Another aspect is that when the person switches chairs, and identifies with the opposite side, his or her nonverbal behavior usually shifts significantly. For instance, in one chair she might be submissive and pleading, while in the other she is commanding and authoritative. Some people alternate between these opposite interpersonal roles in their daily life, while others express only one role, with other people filling the other role. These nonverbal movements, gestures, hesitations, tone of voice, and so on, express much more than the words alone, particularly about the disturbed relationship between the two. This nonverbal expression can be pointed out and explicitly included in the ongoing dialogue and interaction. This provides a wealth of additional information–much of which was initially unconscious–in the process of working toward eventual integration and resolution.

For instance, someone might be talking in a reasonable tone of voice, but with tightly clenched fists. This can be pointed out, and the instruction to "give your fists words" often brings forth anger that had been hidden, but can now participate overtly in the interaction. I can remember Fritz Perls often saying, "I hear your voice drenched with tears," pointing out a tonality that indicated that some sadness needed to be acknowledged or some grieving needed to be completed. Hunched shoulders often indicate an attitude of having given up a struggle, even though the words march on woodenly, like defeated soldiers.

Finally, as the client switches chairs and becomes both sides of the conflict in turn, it becomes evident that both sides are actually within the person. Even when the conflict is between the client and a real person who is still alive, the real conflict is internal, not external. The real person is not in the room; it is the images of that person in the client's mind that is causing the trouble. When the internal conflict is resolved, a person can devote all his effort to meeting the external challenge or difficulty presented by the other person.

Of Two Minds

Even if people are not having a two-chair dialogue, whenever they are experiencing a conflict, they are of "two minds," alternating between responding to what one voice says, and then the other. And since this incongruence will also be expressed physically as they respond to the opposing voices, they will also be of "two bodies." This incongruence of battling opposites is always observable in movements, positions, and gestures that "waffle," alternating between responding to each of the two voices, never quite taking a stand for either one for very long.

For instance, when someone is incongruent about reaching out to another person, her hand will reach forward, and then hesitate or withdraw, or the upper torso may move forward and then back, or the head may move slightly to one side and then the other. This incongruence will also be evident in physical imbalance, since different parts of the body will often tend to move in different directions, rather than as a whole in one direction. This ambivalence will prevent the person from fully committing to any gesture or movement.

In contrast, congruent gestures are definitive; all movements and other nonverbal behaviors completely support whatever the person is experiencing at the time. Whether someone is congruently moving toward or away, laughing, fighting, or loving, all parts are united in expressing it "wholeheartedly."

If two voices are collaboratively discussing a decision, there will also be some evidence of incongruence, as different aspects that are relevant are considered in turn, but it won't be a battle. This kind of incongruence will be less pronounced, and it will be temporary, lasting only as long as the different aspects are separate and haven't yet reached a conclusion or resolution.

For all these reasons, simply opposing a troubling voice by saying, "Shut up!" is a solution that has the serious and inescapable problem of conflict and incongruence. If a client has been a powerless puppet to a dominating voice, allying with the client against the voice by suggesting saying "Shut up!" to the voice could be a useful first step to mobilize the client to deal with the voice. However, the eventual goal should be to resolve the resulting conflict and reach congruence and wholeness. Since opposing a troubling internal voice would add yet another battle to the burden of all the other conflicts that someone already has, it's a very inelegant solution, replacing one problem with another one—which could be worse.

Cognitive-Behavioral Therapy

Next I want to examine a somewhat more refined approach to talking back to a troublesome internal voice. David Burns is a student of Aaron Beck (1987), who is sometimes described as the "father" of Cognitive Ttherapy or Cognitive- Behavioral Ttherapy (CBT, Beck, 1987). CBT has even deeper roots in the work of Albert Ellis (2007), whose work was originally called Rational Therapy, later Rational Emotive Therapy, and finally Rational Emotive Behavior Therapy (Ellis, 2007) as it evolved over the years. As early as the 1950s—over half a century ago—Ellis advocated verbally challenging a client's self-defeating beliefs and behaviors by demonstrating the irrationality, self-defeatism, and rigidity of their negative self-talk. Burns is one of many prominent contemporary Cognitive Behavioral Therapists who advocate countering a troublesome voice with an approach that is somewhat more specific and detailed than Bandler's "Shut up!" Burns writes:

> Talk back to that internal critic! . . .
>
> a. Train yourself to recognize and write down the self-critical thoughts as they go through your mind;
> b. Learn why these thoughts are distorted; and
> c. Practice talking back to them so as to develop a more realistic self-evaluation system." (Burns, 1992, p. 62)

In this process the client is taught how to notice the content of automatic thoughts, identify the kind of distortion, and then generate a rational response. For instance, if the automatic thought is "I never do anything right," the distortion is overgeneralization, and a rational response is, "Nonsense, I do a lot of things right."

"This shows what a jerk I am" is an example of the distortion called labeling, and a rational response is, "Come on, now, I'm not 'a jerk.'"

Although these rational responses are a little gentler than "Shut up!" they still oppose and disagree with the troublesome voice. People in the real world don't like to be disagreed with, and internal voices are no different; they are likely to become defensive, and redouble their efforts to convince you of what they are saying.

Burns developed this method while working with seriously depressed patients who were often suicidal, people who had given up all hope of having a normal, satisfying life. The main symptoms of depression are feelings of hopelessness, helplessness, and worthlessness, and most—if not all—of this is in response to internal voices that criticize, berate, and torment the depressed person. In this context, rallying the client's resources to oppose internal voices is a significant step forward, and research indicates that CBT gets results with depressed people that are superior to antidepressant medication and most other therapies.

Since then, Burns has applied the same method to quite a variety of other problems that result from troublesome internal voices, including anger, guilt, addiction to love and approval, and perfectionism. If someone who is suffering from one of these problems feels completely defeated, then mobilizing a rational response to it can be a useful first step.

Just as Bandler's "Shut up!" method works, Burns's process also works. The important questions are, for whom is it useful, what are the results, and what are the drawbacks? Although Burns's system is more differentiated than Bandler's simple—and rather rude—"Shut up!" it still suffers from all the same problems.

Opposing an automatic thought tends to make it stronger, and it increases the noise in the auditory system, making it difficult for more useful supporting voices to be heard.

Furthermore, in the public demonstrations of CBT that I have seen, the major focus is on the words that are spoken, devoting little or no attention to the nonverbal aspects of the voice—the volume, tone, tempo, and so on. Often the nonverbal messages are far more important in expressing the essence of the voice's communication, particularly the relationship aspect. Bringing them into the dialogue adds a great deal of previously hidden information, as described previously.

But most important, Burns' process, like Bandler's, also inevitably creates conflict and incongruence, and it ignores the positive intent of a troublesome voice. Burns's approach can be a useful first step for someone who is depressed and has totally given up, but it falls far short of the eventual goal of full integration, wholeness, and congruence.

If opposing a troublesome internal voice doesn't work very well, how about an even more radical intervention, trying to silence an internal voice altogether? This is an approach that many spiritual practices have advocated and taught for thousands of years, and one that many widely known contemporary teachers continue to advocate, so it deserves a chapter of its own.

12. Not Silencing an Internal Voice

The first nine chapters of this book present a wide variety of methods that you can use to change a troublesome internal voice and your response to it. You can use them to change an internal troublesome voice into a helpful ally, and modify what it says to you—and how it says it—to make it easier and more useful to listen to. The previous chapter explored the limited usefulness of talking back to a voice or telling it to shut up, and the very significant drawbacks of doing this.

Next I want to briefly review an approach that not only does not work at all, but has even more serious consequences than talking back to a voice. When someone is tormented by an internal voice, often the first response is to want to eliminate it altogether, because it makes the person feel so bad. However, if you have ever tried to eliminate a troublesome voice, you know that it is extremely difficult—if not impossible—to do, as discussed in Chapter 11. In fact, trying to get rid of it draws your attention to it even more and results in making it more powerful, and your unpleasant response to it even stronger. It's very similar to the old joke about trying not to think of pink elephants—they just get bigger, pinker, and more numerous.

The idea of quieting internal voices has been a significant part of Buddhism and many other spiritual practices for thousands of years. Quieting the internal "chattering monkey" has been advocated as a path to reaching enlightenment or nirvana. However, very little has been said about exactly how to actually accomplish this, or what it would be like to experience nirvana. What would it be like to have no internal voices at all? And what would the consequence be? Would it be enlightenment, or something else, or possibly both? Nirvana might come at a significant price.

Fortunately, we have a coherent and detailed first-person account of what it is like to have no internal voices. In 1996, Dr. Jill Bolte Taylor, a neuroanatomist who studied the brain, had a massive stroke when a blood vessel exploded in the left hemisphere of her brain, forming a large blood clot that pressed on her language area, interrupting her ability to generate language, and eventually shutting it down altogether. Even though Dr. Taylor was a brain scientist, she didn't immediately recognize what was happening to her. As her language and other left hemisphere functions gradually shut down, she intermittently entered a state that she described as "euphoria," "nirvana," and "la la land," in which she became less and less able to function. A dozen years later, after her full recovery, she described her experience in a fascinating videotaped TED talk that went "viral" which you can view online (Taylor, 2008). The following excerpts are from the online transcript of that talk:

> And I'm asking myself, "What is wrong with me; what is going on?" And in that moment, my brain chatter, my left hemisphere brain chatter went totally silent. Just like someone took a remote control and pushed the mute button and—total silence.
>
> And at first I was shocked to find myself inside of a silent mind. But then I was immediately captivated by the magnificence of energy around me. And because I could no longer identify the boundaries of my body, I felt enormous and expansive. I felt at one with all the energy that was, and it was *beautiful* there.
>
> Then all of a sudden my left hemisphere comes back online and it says to me, "Hey! We got a problem, we got a problem, we gotta get some help."

As Dr. Taylor drifts back and forth between normal consciousness and the beautiful inner silence, she struggles to telephone a colleague for help:

> I do not understand numbers, I do not understand the telephone, but it's the only plan I have. So I had to wield my paralyzed arm like a stump, and cover the numbers as I went along and pushed them, so that as I would come back to normal reality I'd be able to tell, "Yes, I've already dialed that number." Eventually the whole number gets dialed, and I'm listening to the phone, and my colleague picks up the phone and he says to me, "Whoo woo wooo woo woo." And I think to myself, "Oh my gosh, he sounds like a golden retriever!" And so I say to him, clear in my mind, I say to him, "This is Jill! I need help!" And what comes out of my voice is, "Whoo woo wooo woo woo." I'm thinking, "Oh my gosh, *I* sound like a golden retriever!" So I couldn't know—I didn't know that I couldn't speak or understand language until I tried.

The first thing I want to point out is that Dr. Taylor's report shows how useful her internal voice was in understanding what was happening to her, and in both motivating her to get help, and in carrying out the behaviors to get that help. From "And I'm asking myself, 'What is wrong with me; what is going on?' " to "Oh my gosh, I sound like a golden retriever!" her internal voice directed her attention in ways that were useful in getting help, and probably saving her life.

Dr. Taylor's report is quite similar to the reports of some people who have used hallucinogenic drugs. Others have had similar experiences during epileptic seizures and in other unique situations such as sensory deprivation tanks, which can have profound effects on the brain, and the ability to use language. Perhaps more interesting, the same kind of experience can be created without requiring a stroke, drugs, or extreme environments that affect the ability to hear internal voices.

In an early Neuro-Linguistic Programming workshop in the 1970s, a man who had read far too many books about the value of silencing your inner dialogue used his skills to do exactly that, for a short period of time. When he did this, he experienced total internal silence—and total catatonic immobility. After he returned from this experiment, some exploration revealed that all his behavior began with some kind stimulus and direction from an internal voice, saying something like, "What shall I do next?" or "What's most important now?" Without this internal voice, and its useful prompting, he was immobilized. He was in the here and now all right—just as many stroke victims and Alzheimer's patients are—but he couldn't get anywhere else, and he was totally incapacitated.

So while silencing your internal voices may be interesting as a temporary experiment, it has very significant practical drawbacks. Your internal voice may sometimes be a chattering monkey that criticizes and torments you, but at many other times it is a very valuable ability, one that, as far as we know, no other animal has.

Sometimes a voice just helps you read addresses or phone numbers—an ordinary skill that can be easily ignored and taken for granted, until it's no longer there. As Dr. Taylor discovered, this simple ability can sometimes be very, very important. At other times a pair of internal voices might engage in very useful planning about what restaurant to go to, which car to buy, or whether to get married or not. Without those internal voices, you would be as helpless as Dr. Taylor was. If you were always in the here and now, you would not be able to reminisce about pleasing past events, and you would not be able to plan future ones.

However, quite a number of spiritual traditions, new age movements, and even psychotherapies continue to advocate being in the here and now. As I pointed out in my earlier book (S. Andreas, 2012), this can be a useful way to temporarily withdraw your attention from a troubling problem you are ruminating about, so it has a certain usefulness in that context. However, many have taken this to an extreme, promoting it as a permanent solution to all problems. In the 1960s and 1970s, the idea of being in the now was a key part of many new age programs that were very popular, such as Baba Ram Dass's (1971) book, *Remember, Be Here Now*. One way to be in the here and now—Dr. Taylor's la la land—is to silence the internal voices that so often talk about other times and places in the past or the future. Even when voices talk about the present, those words tend to withdraw attention from present events themselves.

Fritz Perls' Gestalt Therapy (which I was deeply involved in for over 10 years), encounter groups, and many other personal growth methods in the late 1960s and 1970s, were based on becoming aware of events in the moment. If you are tormented by images of the past or future, it is often useful to learn how to return to the present moment as a temporary refuge—unless the present moment is also painful or terrifying. But it can also be very useful and supportive to remember past times that were pleasant, exciting, interesting, or comforting. Imagining a positive future to work toward can also sustain you in enduring a very difficult present. Our brains enable us to travel back to any time in the past that we can remember, and enable us to use our memories to construct an enjoyable future.

Of course we could also use the same time-traveling skill to remember past failures, pains, and ugliness, and use those memories to forecast disappointing and disastrous futures—which is what many depressed people do. The solution is not to eliminate our ability to time travel but to use that skill appropriately, so that it makes our life better, not worse.

In recent years there has been considerable interest in what has been called "mindfulness." Though vaguely defined, mindfulness appears to me to be old wine in new bottles, fundamentally the same as the exhortations to be in the now of the 1960s and 1970s.

If these approaches were more effective in actually achieving what Dr. Taylor experienced, proponents might be a good deal less enthusiastic about it. But since very few get more than a very brief experience of inner silence, the drawbacks aren't so noticeable, and they can continue to pursue their mostly unattainable holy grail.

If we look a bit more closely at those who advocate silencing internal dialogue, we find some very interesting contradictions. I have not heard that even one of them (including Dr. Taylor) has volunteered to have their language area surgically disabled so that they could become aphasic and have Dr. Taylor's experience of nirvana. Nirvana may possibly be a nice destination for a short vacation, but apparently no one wants to live there year-round.

Another contradiction is that if someone's goal is to silence internal dialogue, talking about it adds yet more words for internal dialogue to say, not less—even more words to divert your attention from the here and now. Those who teach spiritual practices are continually warning—with yet more words—about the very real trap of learning how to talk at even greater length about enlightenment, rather than simply experiencing it in silence. To be congruent, their instruction in how to silence an internal voice should be entirely nonverbal, using no words at all.

Eckhart Tolle, the author of *The Power of Now* (Tolle, 2004) and *A New Earth* (Tolle, 2006), is one of many who are currently promoting this ancient idea. He also has many audiobooks and other products. One of Tolle's other books is titled *Stillness Speaks* (Tolle, 2003), a contradiction indicating that for him even stillness has a voice. A CD is titled *Whispers of Now*, another contradiction showing that for Tolle the now also speaks—in a whisper. Furthermore, he couldn't have created all those written books and audio programs if he didn't have a very active internal voice, not the silence that he advocates.

Moreover, if you watch him speak in his many YouTube videos, his frequent blinking and eye movements reveal that while he is talking, he is accessing quite a variety of internal voices and images; he is a good deal less in contact with the here and now than most people are. A YouTube video titled "Honoring Others" is a particularly striking example; watching the video with the sound off makes it easier to notice his frequent eye movements, all of which indicate attending to internal images and voices of the past and future, not anything in the present moment.

In simplified form, what many advocates of internal silence are saying, in words—over and over again—is "Words are useless; get rid of them." If this statement were true, then it would be meaningless, because the statement itself is only a string of useless words. Ram Dass's (1971) book with the title *Remember, Be Here Now* is a curious command to remember to be here now, but if you are remembering, you are not in the here and now. It is also an instruction with the same paradoxical structure—a set of words that tells us to ignore words (but at least the words in his book were poetic, and accompanied by many interesting illustrations). Those instructions all have the same self-contradiction as the sentence, "Don't listen to me."

Chimpanzees don't use words (except for those who have been taught a few by psychologists), but most people don't realize that if they got rid of words, they would become as limited as chimpanzees are. Those who advocate eliminating internal voices really should advertise their goal as attaining "chimpanzee consciousness," "Alzheimer's consciousness," or "aphasic consciousness." And to be congruent, they should do this without using any words. But somehow words like "enlightenment," "unconditioned mind," "nirvana," and other variations on that theme are much better for marketing to the millions of people who are spending hundreds of millions of dollars in a futile self-contradictory quest—to use words (printed or spoken) to try to get rid of words.

By now it should be obvious that silencing all internal voices is a fairly drastic overreaction to a very limited problem, truly throwing out the baby with the bathwater. It is as if people said, "Since some voices are troublesome, let's eliminate all of them—including the useful ones." That is known as an all-or-none solution, something that is all too common, but rarely useful or satisfying.

I hope the deep meaning of the Milton Erickson quotation at the beginning of this book is becoming fully apparent. "Your task is that of altering, not abolishing." You can change many aspects of your inner voices in quite a variety of useful ways, and in this book I have offered you a number of them. But if you try to abolish any part of them, you will only make your problem worse, not better; and if you were to succeed, you would become less human, not more.

Closing

In this book and my previous one (S. Andreas, 2012), I have presented all the ways that I know of to alter a troublesome internal voice. I learned some of these methods long ago, from a number of other people, while others are more recent, and some are refinements of older ones. I am always learning and adapting new methods to discover what works best.

For example, I recently developed a specific adaptation of adding music to a voice, a major topic presented in my previous book. Listen to what your troublesome voice says, and then condense that into a three- to six- word sentence that captures the essence of what it says to you, such as "I'm so stupid." . . .

Now think of a piece of music that is upbeat, triumphant, or inspiring to you in some way. One of my favorites is the "Hallelujah Chorus" of Handel's *Messiah*, but any music that is uplifting for you will work. . . .

Now sing that short sentence very loudly, internally (or externally if you are alone) to the music you have chosen, over and over. You may have to change the words a bit to fit the rhythm of the music. For instance, if you sing the sentence above to the tune of the "Hallelujah Chorus," it might go, "I'mmm . . . so stu-pid; I'mmm . . . so stu-pid, so stu-pid, so stu-pid, so stu-u-pid!" . . .

If that doesn't change your response to the sentence, choose some other uplifting music, and sing your sentence to that music, nice and loud, until you find one that changes your response. . . .

If this becomes an earworm that goes on echoing in the background of your awareness for hours or days, so much the better. That will strengthen your new response to the words and make it almost impossible to hear the sentence in the old way.

As I was revising the manuscript for this book, I discovered Eleanor Longden's report of how the common misunderstanding that hearing voices is a sign of psychosis or other mental illness ruined many years of her life—and nearly ended it. Her story vividly illustrates many of the principles presented in this book, particularly the importance of what kind of relationship you have with an inner voice:

It started when Eleanor was a university student, about to leave a classroom. A clear voice calmly observed, "She is leaving the room." Startled, she looked around but there was no one there. Although hearing this voice was unsettling, its tone was neutral, not criticizing or tormenting, just reporting. This voice persisted, calmly narrating all her behavior.

Then she told a friend about the voice. The friend was horrified and thought something must be seriously wrong, and she insisted that Eleanor get medical attention. Eleanor went to her college G. P., who referred her to a psychiatrist, who also assumed that the voice was a sign of latent insanity. Later she would comment, "I always wish, at this point, the voice had said, 'She is digging her own grave.' "

> A hospital admission followed, the first of many, a diagnosis of schizophrenia came next, and then, worst of all, a toxic, tormenting sense of hopelessness, humiliation and despair about myself, and my prospects. In effect, a vicious cycle of fear, avoidance, mistrust and misunderstanding had been established, and this was a battle in which I felt powerless and incapable of establishing any kind of peace or reconciliation.
>
> Two years later, and the deterioration was dramatic. By now, I had the whole frenzied repertoire: terrifying voices, grotesque visions, bizarre, intractable delusions. My mental health status had been a catalyst for discrimination, verbal abuse, and physical and sexual assault, and I'd been told by my psychiatrist, 'Eleanor, you'd be better off with cancer, because cancer is easier to cure than schizophrenia.' I'd been diagnosed, drugged and discarded, and was by now so tormented by the voices that I attempted to drill a hole in my head in order to get them out.

Then she met a different psychiatrist, and several others who helped her take a more positive attitude toward her voices, seeing them as benign expressions of important aspects of her experience that she had not fully acknowledged, gradually learning to work together in respectful collaboration with the voices.

> Throughout all of this, what I would ultimately realize was that each voice was closely related to aspects of myself, and that each of them carried overwhelming emotions that I'd never had an opportunity to process or resolve, memories of sexual trauma and abuse, of anger, shame, guilt, low self-worth. The voices took the place of this pain and gave words to it, and possibly one of the greatest revelations was when I realized that the most hostile and aggressive voices actually represented the parts of me that had been hurt most profoundly, and as such, it was these voices that needed to be shown the greatest compassion and care. (E. Longden, 2013)

To summarize, Eleanor's initial relationship to her voice was as a neutral companion, but her experience with her horrified friend and alarmed psychiatrist changed this to fear, mistrust, and antagonism, and the voices became louder, more aggressive, and destructive in response. Later others urged her to listen to the voices and make friends with them. When she did this, Eleanor realized that they were alienated aspects of her own experience that needed to be heard, and they gradually became helpful allies.

The methods in this book also have direct applications in many other situations that may not be obvious. For instance, if you have a repetitive symptom that bothers you—a habit, a pain, a physical symptom, a flashback image, or anything else—you can ask it to speak to you, in the same way that you would ask someone in the real world: "If you could speak to me now, what would you say to me? What is your message for me? What would you like me to know?" Whatever it replies to you will be an internal voice, so all the methods in this book can be used to join with it, clarify its message and positive intent, and transform it into a friend and ally. The dialogue that develops may or may not have any impact on the symptom itself, but it can always change your relationship to the symptom. Sometimes that change in relationship is more important than the symptom itself, as it was for Eleanor Longden.

For instance, at 78, my hands are beginning to shake quite a lot, something doctors call "essential tremors." I could easily get upset about this sign of my aging, try to hide it or stop it, and so on. (If I had been a watchmaker, that career would be over!) But I choose to welcome the tremors. I sometimes exaggerate them, and I affectionately call them "my wiggles." That doesn't decrease the wiggles, but it is a lot more pleasant than trying to fight with them.

These processes can also be used with other people in the real world. You can join with a troublesome teenager or boss, and communicate with them in all the ways I have described here, in order to improve your understanding of them and how you relate to them.

I'm sure there must be many other useful adaptations of what I have presented here, additional discoveries and applications for how to modify our internal voices. I invite you to add to what I have presented to enhance your own personal repertoire of self-talk tools.

I want to point out something very important about all the processes I have presented. All of them are very simple processes, like recipes that can easily be followed by someone with very little training or background experience. If you follow the outline of a process, adjusting them to fit the individual, they will work. Period.

As I write this, I have just returned from teaching at a major national psychotherapy conference, where I listened to many well-known therapists talk about their work. Almost all of them spoke in vague terms about the importance of establishing a trusting relationship, helping clients with their capacity for connection, emotional self-regulation, and self-awareness, reducing shame and denial, healing fundamental attachment issues, and a host of other descriptive terms and phrases.

However, very few of them offered any specific processes that would tell someone how to actually accomplish any of those worthwhile goals, and this is generally true of therapy. We need more specific practical processes that can be dependably used to help people change.

If you have tried using the processes I have presented, you will have discovered for yourself how useful they can be. However, some people find the idea of a protocol or recipe for personal change objectionable, and I'd like to respond to two of the major objections I have encountered.

Although it is less true now than in the past, most approaches in the field of psychotherapy have typically maintained that one recipe can be used for all sorts of different human problems. That is like saying that one recipe will work equally well for a beef roast, a chocolate cake, or a tossed salad.

Others make the mistake of confusing the recipe with the result of using the recipe. You can't get any nourishment from the recipe for a casserole, and you can't get much shelter under the architectural plans for a comfortable home. A recipe is only a set of instructions that tells you what to do in order to get a given result. If a recipe is followed carefully, and the appropriate ingredients are available, the result is dependable. Our world is filled with the satisfying results of recipes that work dependably, from cookbooks to computer manuals and cell phones. All of science consists of detailed recipes that get specific results in specified contexts, and the methods described in this book all tell you what to do to get a specific result.

Many years ago, Paul Valery said, "The term science should not be given to anything but the aggregate of the recipes that are always successful. All the rest is literature." Unfortunately, much of psychology is literature—and most of it is not even very good literature. Many years ago, Paul Watzlawick pointed out the very important difference between descriptive language and injunctive language. Art and literature describe how things are in the present. Injunctive language is the language of science; it tells you what to do to get a specific result in the future. Our lives are surrounded by the results of using injunctive language to change and create things.

Descriptive language is exemplified by psychiatry's *DSM-5* diagnostic manual. Over 900 pages describe the different kinds of disorders that people have, but there are only a few vague suggestions about what to do to resolve any of them. Imagine that medical doctors had a manual that only described the immense variety of medical problems that people can have, without any suggestions about what sort of treatment can be used to heal them, and you will have a pretty good representation of the current state of psychotherapy.

In contrast, injunctive language tells you what to do in order to have a particular experience. George Spencer Brown, a mathematician, said it well:

> The taste of a cake, although literally indescribable, can be conveyed to a reader in the form of a set of injunctions called

> a recipe. Music is a similar art form; the composer does not even attempt to describe the set of sounds he has in mind, much less the set of feelings occasioned through them, but writes down a set of commands (a musical score) which, if they are obeyed by the reader, can result in a reproduction, to the reader, of the composer's original experience. (Brown, 2004)

Frieda Fromm-Reichman, a therapist, once said, "People don't come to therapy for explanation; they come for experience." A recipe is a dependable way to create a specific experience. Unfortunately, most current therapies—and there are now over a thousand different named therapies—are still unable to do that dependably. Just as a trained chef can get better results with a recipe than a beginning cook, experience can certainly improve the skill and subtlety of your use of a recipe. However, it doesn't require any complicated theoretical or psychological background. In fact, a good recipe can be used successfully by someone whose understanding is totally lacking, or even completely wrong.

For example, about 25 years ago, my wife and I developed a dependable process to guide a client from anger or resentment to forgiveness (Andreas, 2008) in a modeling seminar that we were teaching. Rather than talk about modeling, we thought it appropriate and congruent to actually do some new modeling in the seminar, and develop a new method. In the forgiveness process the shift from anger or resentment to forgiveness is ridiculously simple and actually takes only seconds.

However, before someone is willing to make this shift, the many objections that most people typically have to forgiving someone else have to be satisfied. "That bastard doesn't deserve forgiveness; if I forgave him that would mean that I condoned what he did to me!" Statements like this presuppose that forgiveness is for the other person, and also that forgiveness is equivalent to condoning.

Until and unless these kinds of objections are satisfied, an angry person will be steadfast in being unwilling to even consider forgiveness as an option, and therapy will be long, tedious, expensive, and unrewarding. Objections are fairly easy to satisfy if you have some experience with the major kinds of objection that someone is likely to have to the resolution of a given problem, and if you have thought through and rehearsed appropriate responses.

Sometime after we first published our process for forgiveness and produced an audiotaped demonstration, I saw an advertisement for an audiotape on forgiveness, so I ordered it out of curiosity, to see what I might learn. What I learned was that the author of the tape had "borrowed" our entire process, word for word, without giving any credit. He began the tape describing a very complicated theory about how the process worked that had no relationship whatsoever to our understanding of it. However, when he used our recipe to guide a woman through the process, she was successful in reaching forgiveness. I took that as a supreme compliment to the process that we had developed—that someone with no understanding of the process whatsoever could guide someone through it successfully.

Very few people will ever approach the level of skill and subtlety that Milton Erickson or Virginia Satir achieved. It took them many decades of very dedicated practice, relentless creative experimentation, and total openness to feedback about what worked and what didn't. Most therapists are not willing or able to sustain that level of determination and commitment to learning.

Beginning therapists who have clear and dependable protocols or recipes to follow can often get the same kind of results as Erickson and Satir—and in some cases better and faster than those master therapists achieved. They may not be able to do it as artfully or gracefully, but they can usually do it a lot faster, and cheaper.

Some people think that slavish imitation of a master is the best way to honor their creativity and skill. But in any field of science, the best way to honor a pioneer is to improve on what he or she did. As Sir Isaac Newton—a giant himself—said, "If I have seen further, it is by standing on the shoulders of giants." Newton apparently borrowed this idea from the 12th-century theologian and author John of Salisbury, who used a version of the phrase in a treatise on logic called *Metalogicon*, written in Latin in 1159. Translations of this difficult book are quite variable, but the gist of what Salisbury said is, "We are like dwarfs sitting on the shoulders of giants. We see more, and things that are more distant, than they did, not because our sight is superior, or because we are taller than they, but because they raise us up, and by their great stature add to ours."

My old teacher Fritz Perls used to say, "Just because you have a chisel doesn't make you Michelangelo." On the other hand, if Michelangelo hadn't had any chisels, how could he have released the sublime visions imprisoned within those stolid blocks of marble?

The methods in this book are precision tools that people can use to find release—and relief—from their prisons; practice them, and learn how to use them well, and that will be the greatest thanks you could offer me.

Appendix 21 Steps to Transform a Troublesome Inner Voice

A verbatim transcript showing how to use this process appears in Chapter 8.

If you do this exercise by yourself, close your eyes and pause after reading each step of the instructions, so that you can fully reenter your experience of the previous step before doing what the instructions ask you to do next. You will have to open your eyes periodically to read the instructions for the next step, which will tend to interrupt your experiencing. It will be much easier, and the results will usually be better, if you have a friend who can read the instructions to you in a soft slow voice, and pause while you complete each step, so that you can focus completely on doing the process without interruption.

If a second friend is available, she or he can be a coach, following the outline along with the guide, making occasional suggestions to the guide, or to you directly, based on observation of the guide's instructions, your responses, and the interaction between you.

1. Select voice. "Remember a troublesome internal voice that has criticized you or your behavior in the present moment, reminded you of past failures or embarrassments, or foretold future failure, and so on." . . .
2. Listen to the voice. "Now listen carefully to the sound of this voice—the tonality, volume, tempo, hesitations, and so on, that you hear—all the qualities that allow you to recognize someone's voice on the phone instantly, out of all the thousands of voices you have heard." . . .
3. Identify voice. "Whose voice is this? Is it your voice or someone else's?" . . .

   If it is someone else's voice, go directly to step 4, below.

   If it is your own voice, ask, "Who did you learn from to talk in this way?" . . .

   If you can't identify the voice, ask, "If you did know, who would it be?" or "Who does this voice remind you of?"
4. Add image of person. "As you hear this voice, see the person who is speaking to you, and watch all their facial movements, expressions, gestures, and so on, to find out what else you can learn about their experience as they talk to you." . . .
5. See larger context. "Now expand the scope of what you see and hear to include the larger context in both space and time. Where are you, and what just happened that this person is responding to? View this event in detail, including what happened earlier that was relevant to this event, and also what happened later as a result, in order to understand it more fully and completely." . . .

6. Notice speaker's limitations. "Notice what that person was simply unable to do because of their upbringing, beliefs, frustrations, or other inadequacies or limitations. Realize that both what they said, and how they said it, may have had very little to do with you, and a great deal to do with their difficulty in communicating clearly and directly." . . .
7. Clarify message. "Would you please clarify your message? What would you say to me if you had been able to express yourself fully, and talk honestly about more of your experience of this situation? What is it that you really want me to hear?" . . .
8. Give thanks for any clarification. "Thank you for clarifying your communication." . . .

   If the communication is still unclear, ask again—as many times as necessary, thanking the voice for each response—until the communication is clear to you.
9. Ask for the positive intent. "What is your positive intent in telling me this?" If the response doesn't appear to be positive, ask for the intent of this intent. "Thank you. What is your positive intent in telling me that?" You may need to ask several times before you receive an answer that you think is positive, and that you can agree with. Usually the positive intent is some kind of protection, either for you, the voice, or a third person or group of people. . . .
10. Give sincere thanks for the positive intent. "Thanks very much for telling me your positive intent." . . .

    Then ask, "Would you be willing to consider communicating in a different way, so that it would be much easier for me to pay full attention to what it is that you want me to hear?" . . .

    Usually you will get a "yes" answer, because this proposed change supports the voice's positive intent in communicating with you even better than what it had been doing. If you get a "no" answer, that means that there has been some miscommunication. Back up one or more steps and clarify the miscommunication before moving forward again. . . .
11. Pause to examine the positive intent. Notice whether the positive intent was only for you, or for the person speaking to you, or for someone else, or some combination of these three basic alternatives.
12. List voice's special abilities. Make a list of this person's special skills and abilities, and then compliment them. "You are really good at ________ and ________."
13. Identify the skills that you learned. Go through the list you made and notice which of this person's skills you have learned, and give appreciation for what you have learned—even if the process of learning it might have been unpleasant. "I learned well from you how to ________ and ________. Thanks very much for teaching me that."

14. Identify the skills that you didn't learn. Again, go through the list you made and notice which of this person's skills you didn't learn, and give appreciation. "You are also really good at ________ and ________, and I never learned how to do that well."
15. Ask if the voice would like to assist you. "Would you be willing to assist me in situations where those skills would be useful to me?" . . .

    Assuming that it says yes, test by thinking of a past situation in which you could have used that kind of assistance, and find out what the voice says to you. . . .

    Assuming that goes well, imagine a future situation in which you might be able to use that kind of assistance, and find out what the voice says to you. . . .

    (Optional) If the voice is still somewhat difficult to listen to, and you would like to modify it so that it is more comfortable for you to hear, continue with the following steps.
16. Identify a trusted friend. "Think of a special friend of yours—either in the present or in the past—of the same sex as the voice, who you know cares for you and has positive intentions, someone whom you would listen to carefully, no matter what she or he said." . . .

    If you can't find one, ask, "If I did have such a trusted friend, what would that person's voice sound like?" . . .
17. Listen to this friend's voice. "Listen to the qualities of this person's voice—its tonality, volume, tempo, hesitations, and so on, and particularly notice the unique qualities that distinguish this voice from all the other voices you have ever heard." . . .
18. Adopt the tonality of the friend's voice. Ask this voice that has been troubling you, "Would you be willing to try using this voice of my trusted friend, whom I would listen to attentively no matter what it said? I am not suggesting taking away any old choices, only offering a new one. If I don't listen well, you can always go back to using the voice that you have used in the past." . . .

    If the voice doesn't agree to this, there must have been some misunderstanding at an earlier step; back up one or more steps to clarify this before going forward again.
19. Testing. Assuming that the troublesome voice agrees, ask, "Please try out using that voice right now, to find out how well it works." . . .

    Assuming that it does so, notice how you respond differently, and thank the voice sincerely for being willing to make this change. . . .

    If you think it would be useful, ask the voice to make any further adjustments that you'd like to make in how it speaks to you using your friend's voice. For instance, if the voice is too loud, you could ask it to speak a bit more softly. Or perhaps you'd like to adjust when it communicates with you, so that it talks to you before some activity, or afterward, but not during the activity because that would distract you from what you are doing, and so on. . . .

20. Rehearsal and testing. "Think of a future situation in which this voice might have something useful to say to you, and find out what happens." . . .

    If the test is not satisfactory, back up one or more steps to modify how or when the voice speaks to you, and then come forward again.

21. Congruence check. "Does any part of me have any objection or concern about any of the changes that have been made?" . . .

    If you notice anything in response to this question, in any sensory modality (feelings, images, words, or sounds) first discover whether or not it is actually an objection. Talk directly to the sensation: "If you have an objection to the arrangements we have made, please increase that sensation; if you have no objection, allow the sensation to diminish," and find out what happens. If there is an increase, indicating an objection, then do whatever is necessary to clarify what the objection is. "Please allow that feeling to transform into an image or set of words that will clarify what your objection is." Then satisfy the objection in order to reach agreement and remove any interference with the changes that have been made.

There are three different fundamental ways to satisfy an objection:

a. Adjust the change so that it no longer interferes with one or more other important outcomes that you have. "Choose the voice of a different trusted friend, and find out if that works better for you."
b. Carefully contextualize the change so that it doesn't occur in any context in which it might interfere with some other important outcome. "This change might only be appropriate in your personal life, not in your professional life, where it could cause trouble."
c. Reframe or recategorize the meaning of either the change or the objection to the change, so that there is no longer any conflict between their outcomes. "You object to having this person speaking using your friend's voice because you think you might lose track of reality. But actually it is a sign of your creativity and flexibility; crazy people are very rigid and uncreative. And as long as you don't tell anyone else about this voice, it won't concern them."

Or, of course, you can use any combination of the three kinds of modification above—either simultaneously or sequentially.

References

Andreas, C., & Andreas, S. (1989). *Heart of the mind: Engaging your inner power to change with neuro-linguistic programming.* Boulder, CO: Real People Press.

Andreas, M. (2010). *Sweet fruit from the bitter tree: 61 true stories of creative and compassionate ways out of conflict.* Boulder, CO: Real People Press.

Andreas, S. (1991). *Virginia Satir: The patterns of her magic.* Boulder, CO: Real People Press.

Andreas, S. (2000). Forgiveness. Steve Andreas, http://steveandreas.com/Articles/forgiveness.html.

Andreas, S. (2002). *Transforming your self: Becoming who you want to be.* Boulder, CO: Real People Press.

Andreas, S. (2006a). *Six blind elephants: Understanding ourselves and each other* (Vols. 1 & 2). Boulder, CO: Real People Press.

Andreas, S. (2006b). Transforming troublesome internal voices [audiotape]. Phoenix, AZ: Milton Erickson Foundation. BT06-W32.

Andreas, S. (2010). You're not good enough [client session video]. Boulder, CO: Real People Press.

Andreas, S. (2012). *Transforming negative self-talk: Practical, effective exercises.* New York: Norton.

Andreas, S., & Andreas, C. (1987). *Change your mind—and keep the change.* Boulder, CO: Real People Press.

Andreas, S., & Andreas, C. (2002) Resolving Grief http://www.steveandreas.com/Articles/grief02.html

Andreas, S., & Dilts, R. (2008). Working with belief systems [audiotape]. Phoenix, AZ: Milton Erickson Foundation. BT08 Dialogue 05.

Bandler, R. (2008). *Get the life you want.* Deerfield Beach, FL: Health Communications.

Beck, A. T. (1987). *Cognitive therapy of depression.* New York: Guilford.

Brown, G. S. (2004). *Laws of form.* Leipzig, Germany: Bohmeier.

Burns, D. (1992). *Feeling good: The new mood therapy.* New York: Avon.

Dass, B. R. (Richard Alpert). (1971). *Remember, be here now.* San Cristobal, NM: Lama Foundation.

Ellis, A. (2007). *Overcoming resistance: A rational emotive behavior therapy integrated approach.* New York: Springer.

Farrelly, F., & Brandsema, J. (1974). *Provocative therapy.* Capitola, CA: Meta.

Flemons, D. (2002). *Of one mind: The logic of hypnosis, the practice of therapy.* New York: Norton.

Flemons, D. (2004). Embodying the mind and minding the body: Using hypnosis in brief therapy. In S. Madigan (Ed.), *Therapeutic conversations 5: Therapy from the outside in.* Vancouver, BC: Yaletown Family Therapy.

Lakoff, G. (1987). *Women, fire, and dangerous things: What categories reveal about the mind*. Chicago: University of Chicago Press.

Longden, E. (2013, August). The voices in my head. TED talk video and transcript. http://www.ted.com/talks/eleanor_longden_the_voices_in_my_head.html.

Newhart, B. (2010). Stop it [video]. YouTube.

Perls, F. (1969a). *Gestalt therapy verbatim*. Gouldsboro, ME: Gestalt Journal Press.

Perls, F. (1969b). *In and out the garbage pail*. Gouldsboro, ME: Gestalt Journal Press.

Stevens, J. O. (1970). *Awareness: Exploring experimenting, experiencing*. Gouldsboro, ME: Gestalt Journal Press.

Taylor, J. B. (2006). Jill Bolte Taylor's stroke of insight. TED talk video and transcript. http://www.ted.com/talks/jill_bolte_taylor_s_powerful_stroke_of_insight.html.

Tolle, E. (2003). *Stillness speaks: Whispers of now*. Novato, CA: New World Library.

Tolle, E. (2004). *The power of now: A guide to spiritual enlightenment*. Novato, CA: New World Library.

Tolle, E. (2006). *A new earth: Awakening to your life's purpose*. New York: Penguin.

Van Dusen, W. (1996). *Returning to the source: The way to the experience of God*. Boulder, CO: Real People Press.

Index